Children's Curriculum

For Use with:

G. H. Construction Crew
Children's Journal

Critter County Clubhouse
Children's Activity Book

CONSTRUCTION ZONE

Developed by Scottie May

Written by Cindy Kenney

Critter County stories by Paula Bussard

Critter County songs by Christine Wyrtzen

Important Information

The Chapel of the Air Ministries is not responsible for situations arising from the use of this curriculum by churches, groups, or individuals.

Children's Curriculum: Grades 1–6
Developer: Scottie May
Writer: Cindy Kenney
Critter County Story Writer: Paula Bussard
Songwriter: Christine Wyrtzen
Editors: Debbie Bible and Jeanette Dall
Cover Illustrations: Bethany Hissong
Cover Design: Bethany Hissong
Text Design: Blum Graphic Design
Text Illustrations: Larry Nolte
Adventure Series Editor: Marian Oliver

Printed in the United States of America.

The Chapel Ministries is a nonprofit, nondenominational, international Christian outreach dedicated to helping God's church grow spiritually and numerically by revitalizing its members, whether they be gathered or scattered, to be a force for kingdom purposes worldwide. To support this goal, The Chapel Ministries provides print and media resources including the annual 50-Day Spiritual Adventure and the 4-Week Worship Celebration, the daily half-hour television program "You Need to Know," and seasonal radio programming. Year-round Bible study guides are offered through a Joint Ministry Venture with Scripture Union U.S.A., to encourage the healthy spiritual habits of daily Scripture reading and prayer.

CRITTER COUNTY is a registered trademark of Loveland Communications, Inc. Used by permission. Critter County was codeveloped by Paula Bussard and Christine Wyrtzen through their ministry called Loveland Communications. Their books and tapes have been enjoyed by more than a million children across North America. For additional product or concert information, contact Loveland Communications, Inc., Box 8, Loveland, OH 45140, (513) 575-4300.

ISBN 1-57849-016-2

Table of Contents

▶ WHAT IS THIS 50-DAY ADVENTURE CURRICULUM FOR CHILDREN ALL ABOUT? ◀

It's about helping children
- experience the Bible in a new and exciting way.
- learn about life in Bible times.
- discover how they can help to make the body of Christ all God wants it to be.
- learn to love the Lord and his Word.

HOW CAN I HELP CHILDREN DO THIS?

Through the Teaching Methods You Use

There have been many studies done to help us understand how children learn best. Most of these studies show that information learned solely by memorization is forgotten quickly. Therefore, it is our belief that kids learn best when they are actively involved in body, mind, and spirit in the teaching process. To do this effectively, every child who comes to church or church club should be made to feel welcome—and that means more than just greeting a child at the door with a smile. Teachers need to give kids the opportunity to investigate information that interests them, draw their own conclusions based on the truths of the Bible, and then show what they've learned in a creative manner. This is learning through experience, the teaching approach you'll find used in each of the eight Adventure lessons included in this curriculum. For example:

• Through Bible-time projects, kids are given the opportunity to discover for themselves what it must have been like to live in Bible times. They are allowed to work alone or with their friends and at their own pace.

• Through the use of creative drama, Bible Story Time becomes more than mere storytelling in its ability to pull kids into the events being portrayed.

• Through the use of small group discussions, children are given the opportunity to figure out for themselves how to apply to their own lives the Bible story truths they've learned. Talking and praying with the same small group each week fosters the growth of friendships and trust.

Through Teamwork and Creativity

Children aren't the only ones to benefit from this less-teacher-directed instructional style. When teachers don't have to remember a long list of things to say or do next, they have more time to relate to the children. Teachers can watch and listen to children and ask questions. The lesson format makes it easy to divide and share leadership responsibilities among several adults, as well as utilize individual talents more effectively. For example, some leaders will work on administrative duties while others will supervise a Bible-time project, participate in acting out the Bible story, or lead a small group (this needs to be an eight-week commitment). And if an individual wishes to be involved in all three parts, he or she may do that.

While the presentation of the materials is clear, they are a breath of fresh air for individuals who long to put their own creative spin on what they teach. Each activity in this guide should be thought of as a suggestion only. Add or substitute your own creative ideas.

WHO CAN USE THIS CURRICULUM?

This Adventure curriculum material can be used as a weekend children's church or church school program, a midweek program, or a combination thereof. (Information on using this curriculum in different settings starts on p. 19.) It is designed for kids in grades 1–6 but can be adapted for younger children as well. The program can work for any size group and any size church. (Special tips for adapting the curriculum to your church size are included on pgs. 20–22.)

To see this program in action, ask your Adventure coordinator to loan you a copy of the *Getting Ready to Adventure Video*. It contains a children's curriculum segment with footage from a church that tested lessons like those in this guide.

HOW MAY THIS CURRICULUM BE DIFFERENT FROM OTHERS I'VE USED?

This approach to teaching will require more preparation and work than traditional approaches. But, most of the work happens before the Adventure begins. You will need to assign storytellers, small group leaders, and project leaders. You will also need to decide on Bible-time projects and gather materials.

Because no one person is responsible for the whole session, you're likely to get more volunteers, and the work can be spread around. For example, if there are men in your church who are skilled at woodworking, they might enjoy working with children on the Bible-time projects that involve woodworking. The best way to make this program successful is to start getting ready for it at least six to eight weeks in advance.

WHAT CURRICULUM MATERIALS DO I NEED?

This curriculum and the cassette tape *Bible Memory Toolbox* are the most important materials you will need. Recording artist Christine Wyrtzen has written songs based on all of the Bible Blueprint Verses the kids will learn during this Adventure. This fun audiocassette may be used as a sing-along help during song time. (Information for ordering this *Bible Memory Toolbox* tape is on p.128.) In addition, there are other resources available that will help make your Adventure a successful and memorable one.

There are two children's books available for home use. For kids in grades 3–6, there is a journal called *G. H. Construction Crew*. For grades K–2, there's an Adventure activity book called *Critter County Clubhouse*. If you want a lesson to stick for a lifetime, it needs to be reinforced. Kids who use these resources will be more likely to acquire learning that lasts than those who don't use the books.

Both of these books provide the kids with daily activities to help them understand and apply the weekly Adventure topics. If your church hasn't purchased a supply of these books to distribute, make certain the children and their parents know how to get a copy. Check with your church's Adventure coordinator for details, or see page 128 in this curriculum. Although these two books are designed for home use, each week the children will be asked a question based on their journals during Small Group Time.

There is also a music cassette provided for home use. It is also titled *Critter County Clubhouse* and was recorded by Christine Wyrtzen. This tape contains the same songs as *Bible Memory Toolbox*, but the *Clubhouse* tape also includes a Critter County storyline. It is intended to complement the *Critter County Clubhouse* Activity Book for K–2. For ordering information, contact your church's Adventure coordinator, or see page 128 in this guide.

▶ HOW IS THE PROGRAM ORGANIZED? ◀

The children's curriculum focuses on the same topics as the Adult and Student 50-Day Adventure materials. In this guide the weekly Adventure themes are called On-the-Job Training Topics. In addition, children will learn about eight Action Steps. Here's an overview:

Week	On-the-Job Training Topics	Action Step
1	Care for each other in God's family	Listen to others the way Jesus would
2	Get the word out to your friends	Say good things about your church
3	Open the door	Be caring and make a new friend
4	Use your tools well	Put your talents to use
5	Take out the trash	Clean up garbage thoughts and actions
6	Help in other places	Take care of the world and its people
7	Meet with the Master Builder	Meet God through prayer and praise
8	Celebrate the best club ever	Give thanks that Jesus is alive

The program contains eight weekly sessions that are broken down into three major sections: Bible-Time Projects, Bible Story Time, and Life Application (Small Group Time). Additional material has been provided for adaptation to Children's Church Worship and Midweek Programming. The following list of information will give you a brief overview of the session segments and their purposes. A more in-depth explanation of how the weekly sessions work is included for Bible-Time Projects, Bible Story Time, and Small Group Time on pages 15–18.

THREE MAJOR SECTIONS

Bible-Time Projects

Children choose from a variety of projects to work on. Each one teaches about life in Bible times.

Bible Story Time

Children gather together for a presentation that deepens their Bible knowledge and understanding. This section includes:

- Weekly Activities
- Setting the Scene
- Bible Story Presentation
- Comprehension Questions
- Bible Blueprint Memory Verse

Life Application

Children meet in small groups to discuss the Bible story and its application to life. Through conversation and prayer they deepen their relationships with each other and God. This section includes:

- Kid Talk
- Prayer Talk

ADDITIONAL ACTIVITIES FOR CHILDREN'S CHURCH WORSHIP OR MIDWEEK PROGRAMS

Children's Church Worship

This weekly section includes:

- Singing
- Critter County Story
- Offering
- Praise and Prayer

Midweek Extras

This weekly section includes:

- Game
- Singing
- Critter County Story

Children may move through the three main parts of a lesson in any way you choose. For example, the routine could be something like this:

1. Check-in	**OR**	1. Check-in
2. Bible-Time Projects		2. Bible Story Time
3. Bible Story Time		3. Life Application
4. Life Application		4. Bible-Time Projects
5. Dismissal		5. Dismissal

If you decide to use this curriculum for Children's Church Worship or during a Midweek Program, refer to weekly sections titled "Children's Church Worship" and "Midweek Extras." Objectives for each weekly session include the eight Action Steps and eight On-the-Job Training Topics mentioned on page 7. One Action Step and one Training Topic are highlighted each week.

HOW LONG DO I SPEND ON EACH PART OF THE SESSION?

The amount of time you allot to each segment of a session is up to you. Each week's session can be used as a one-hour or two-hour program or something in between. The following chart shows how churches might allot time to four different program settings. These are just suggestions and may be altered as needed.

Session Segments	Sunday School	Children's Church	Midweek Program	Combined Sunday School/ Children's Church
Bible-Time Projects	20 min.	15 min.	40 min.	40 min.
Bible Story Time	20 min.	15 min.	25 min.	25 min.
Life Application	20 min.	15 min.	25 min.	25 min.
Worship Time	_____	15 min.	_____	25 min.
Midweek Extras	_____	_____	30 min.	10 min. (Game)

Ready to Begin—Administrative Information

(See p. 25 for photocopy permission.)

WHAT PREPLANNING NEEDS TO BE DONE?

Plan to have one coordinator for each of the three main parts of each session: Bible Story Time, Bible-Time Projects, and Life Application. Six to eight weeks before beginning the Adventure you will need to have a planning meeting with the people who will be involved in making this Adventure happen. This will include: the administrator, storytellers and story actors, small group leaders, and project planners and leaders. Because the majority of the work is done before the Adventure begins, this organizational meeting is crucial for insuring the success of your program. If you are in a large or small church, see the section titled "How Can the Materials Be Adapted for Use in Small and Large Churches?" on pages 20–22.

WHAT ARE THE DUTIES OF THE STAFF?

Bible-Time Project Leader(s) will:

• Determine how many projects to offer. One project should be made available for every 10 to 12 kids.
• Decide which projects to offer and for how many weeks.
• Provide research materials that will equip students to complete each project.
• Gather materials needed to accomplish each project.
• Supervise each activity.
• Oversee project cleanup.
• Store projects and materials between sessions.

Bible Story Time Leader(s) will:

• Welcome children to the story time.
• Set the scene.
• Lead into and/or participate in the story-telling presentation.

• Ask comprehension questions as a follow-up.
• Present the Bible Blueprint Verses.

Small Group Leader(s) will:

• Sit with their group of six to eight children during the story presentation.
• Meet with their group at the end of each session.
• Build a supportive relationship with the kids.
• Help children apply Bible truths and Action Steps to their own lives by working through the Life Application Pages in this guide.
• Touch base with children in their group during project time.

Administrative Leader(s) will:

• Keep attendance.
• Provide name tags.
• Provide maps, routing, and signs.
• Provide necessary material that may be photocopied.

HOW WILL I DIVIDE THE CHILDREN INTO GROUPS?

Before the Adventure begins, divide the kids into small groups of six to eight members. (This same group of six to eight will stay together throughout the Adventure. They will meet weekly with their small group leader during each session.) You may divide them by grade, by gender, or divide them randomly. Keep in mind that the children in grades K–2 have a different journal at home than the kids in grades 3–6. Though they don't bring their journals to church, the kids will talk about them during the small group discussion times.

WHERE WILL I PUT THE KIDS FOR THE DIFFERENT PARTS OF THE SESSIONS?

 ### Bible-Time Projects

Bible-time work sites are set up to accommodate 10 to 12 kids each. Each site should be stocked with suitable reference materials and supplies, as well as provide the needed work space to complete each project. They can be set up as various stations in a large room setting, or they can take place in a number of smaller rooms where traffic can flow through easily. If you choose to run the 50-Day Adventure in a more traditional weekend church setting, you will need only one room.

It would be wise to use permission slips for the Bible-time projects. Refer to the sample on page 127 for ideas you can adapt to your situation.

 ### Bible Story Time

If possible, bring all of the kids together in one large group for the Bible story presentation. Try to create a casual, non-school-like atmosphere for the Adventure sessions. If possible, have the kids sit on the floor in a carpeted room, on area rugs that can be rolled up, or on carpet squares. If you are limited in space and the Bible-time projects have been set up in your large group area, move the project worktables to the sides or back of the room to make the seating space you need. You may also want to decorate the area to look like a construction site.

 ### Life Application

Small Group Locations

Select interesting and unusual places for the small groups to meet. Small places in and around the building that will have a hideout or clubhouse feel to them work best. You could even consider putting up freestanding tents in the classroom. Other places might include the corner of a hallway, a stage, empty space under a stairwell, or even separate corners of your large group area. Make sure that kids know where the nearest exits are in case of an emergency. Pick areas that are somewhat close to the large group area. The kids should be able to get to their small group locations quickly. Encourage the kids to sit on the floor in a circle so they can talk to each other freely.

HOW DO I ORGANIZE THE WEEKLY SESSIONS?

Attendance

Position your attendance table(s) in a convenient place near the main entrance. Keep in mind that kids will need to be able to line up without causing a traffic jam. Hang a sign or banner that says "G. H. Construction Crew Check-in Here!" or "The 50-Day Adventure Starts Here!" on the front of the table or the wall behind it. If you have a large number of kids to check in, you may want to set up more than one table to speed up the process. You can color code the check-in sites to correspond with the kids' colored name tags, as described in the following section.

Use whatever method of record keeping best fits your situation. If your group is small in number, you can keep one large attendance chart for everyone. If it is a large group, you might prefer to keep separate attendance charts or books for each small group. This will work particularly well if you choose to group the children by their normal class or grade divisions.

The children should check in each week

upon arrival to record their attendance and pick up their name tags. Ask an adult or dependable teen to work at the same attendance table each week.

Name Tags

Color-coded name tags are very effective for helping the kids quickly locate their small groups each week as well as learn other people's names. (They help the adults, too.) In addition to a child's name and his or her group's color, a name tag can include the group leader's name and the location where the small group meets. This is especially helpful in large churches where newcomers may need some extra help finding where they belong. Be sure to provide name tags for all the adults taking part in the program. The small group leaders could wear the same color name tags as their assigned kids.

You can purchase adhesive-backed or plastic folder name tags at an office supply store. Color code them by using different colors of paper or different colored markers to write the names. Ask the group leaders to gather the name tags at the end of each week's session for reuse the next week.

Small Group Names

Although you could simply refer to the groups by their color names, you might want to add to the Adventure by letting the kids select a name for their own group. If possible, have the names relate to the construction theme of this year's Adventure. Or you can choose names such as the twelve tribes of Israel, cities in the New Testament, or the names of the disciples.

Transitions and Traffic Flow

In order to prevent chaos, you need to think things through ahead of time when planning to move groups of children from one place to another. For example, at the end of the Bible Story Time when you are about to dismiss the kids to their small groups, it's a lot less chaotic if you dismiss the groups one at a time with thought to their destinations. Let the groups who have the longest walk leave first. Make the "Rules of the Road" perfectly clear during the first session. If the kids need to be quiet as they pass certain locations, let them know that before they get there. If they need to stay with their leader and not rush ahead, make that clear too. Kids will usually give you the behavior you expect if you make your expectations clear.

Ready to Begin—Weekly Leader Information

(See p. 25 for photocopy permission.)

This section will be a walk-through of one weekly session in detail. Refer to Session One starting on page 51 for more help in understanding the weekly sessions.

WHAT IS THE OVERVIEW?

For your convenience, an overview box is printed at the top of the first page of each session. It is intended to give you a quick picture of the session's On-the-Job Training Topic, Action Step, Bible story basis, and memory verse (sometimes referred to as the Bible Blueprint Verse). This will allow you to quickly check what's coming up in the session as well as review what's already been presented. Here's a sample from Week One:

WEEK ONE

▶ **OVERVIEW** ◀

On-the-Job Training Topic: Care for each other in God's family

Action Step: Listen to others the way Jesus would

Bible Story: Acts 2:42–47; Acts 4:32–35

Memory Verse: 1 John 4:11 (NIV)

WHAT DO THE TEACHING/LEARNING COMPONENTS LOOK LIKE IN DETAIL?

 Bible-Time Projects

The Bible-time projects may be done at the beginning of each weekly session or at the end. But there are a few distinct advantages to using them first. The projects can be set up and ready to go at least 20 minutes before the official start of your sessions. That way the kids who arrive early, such as the children of the program staff members, will have a learning activity to do right away.

Carefully watch the time allotted to project time. Let the kids know the first week that they will have many weeks to finish their projects. Explain cleanup responsibilities, and be sure to cue them when it is time to put things away and gather for Bible Story Time or leave to go home. More information on Bible-time projects is included in this curriculum on pages 27–50.

Bible Story Time

Setup

The story or lesson during the 50-Day Adventure can be presented at the start or during the middle of your session. If you offer the story first, you may wish to include some of the songs by Christine Wyrtzen included in the sing-along cassette, *Bible Memory Toolbox*. That way you can offer music as a welcome, and stragglers won't miss the story.

The drama lesson is designed to be presented by costumed storytellers, play actors, or puppets. If your facility will permit and you so choose, bring all of the kids together in one large group for the Bible story presentation. The members of each small group should sit with their leader. This scatters the adults throughout the whole group, making discipline easier. If there are a lot of children in your program, it's helpful to have the small group leaders gather up their kids and bring them to the story area.

You may or may not choose to create scenery to enhance your storytelling dramas. Some of the Bible-time projects offer activities in scene creation that can be used for the dramas. A simple "stage" area could include a clubhouse or church building. Cardboard signs can be hung from the ceiling or attached to a wall. Additional suggestions can be found in each session's "Setting the Scene" section.

Five Main Activities

A. WEEKLY GREETING

Open with a few welcoming comments and announcements, birthday recognition, and the collection of an offering. (If you are using this curriculum for children's church, you may prefer to wait until your worship time to collect an offering.) Just remember to keep these opening activities brief.

B. SETTING THE SCENE

During the first week's session, you may use the "Setting the Scene" time to explain what the Adventure is about. Then in the following weeks, it can be used to review the previous week's On-the-Job Training Topic (weekly theme) or Action Step and to prepare the kids for the Bible story presentation. Once again, you'll need to remember to keep this section short. (Please note that the general instructions for this section are printed in regular type and the suggestions for things you might say to the kids are printed in **bold** type.)

C. BIBLE STORY PRESENTATION

Many of the Adventure Bible stories are written as skits for one to four adults. If you choose to present the story to the combined group rather than to individual classes, you will need to recruit fewer people to act as storytellers/dramatists. Four or five adults or teens can take turns handling the responsibility. That way the same people won't have to present the Bible story every week. Of course, if you have other ideas on how to present the

Bible story, please feel free to put them into action! The material in this curriculum is meant to spark your creativity, not to limit it.

Encourage your storytellers to try to act and talk like the New Testament characters they're portraying. Encourage them to learn their lines well enough to perform them without a script in hand. If you have difficulty recruiting people who are willing and able to do this, you can revise the scripts so that they are read by a narrator while other individuals mime the action. You can also revise the stories slightly so that the characters can hold their scripts on clipboards or scrolls.

The use of costumes is recommended. A simple way to imitate Bible-time clothing is to take a length of fabric (plain or striped) about 8' x 4', cut a hole for the head in the center, and tie the waist with a scarf, necktie, or rope. A pair of sandals and a headband or scarf will add the finishing touches. Since one of the activities suggested for "Bible-Time Projects" is to have the children make a Bible-time wardrobe, you could ask the kids working at that project station to make the costumes.

While you want to encourage the characters to be natural and adlib a bit, they need to be mindful of time. The skits are intended to be presented in five to ten minutes. To help your storytellers keep within the time limit, make certain there is a clock within their view or arrange for someone to give them a signal when it's time to wrap things up.

D. COMPREHENSION QUESTIONS

In order to help you get a feel for what the children have learned from the story presentation, this curriculum includes comprehension questions to use as a follow-up to each ses-

sion's story. These are just a few direct questions to make sure the kids understand the main points of the Bible story. Be certain to allow the kids time to think before answering each question, but keep in mind that a large group is not the best setting for holding a full-scale discussion with kids. Save the application discussion for Small Group Time.

E. BIBLE BLUEPRINT VERSES

This is the time kids will be introduced to the Adventure Bible memory verses. Each verse is related to the weekly On-the-Job Training Topic and Action Step. As added fun during the Bible Story Time, a volunteer will be given the chance to use a construction tool to get to the Bible verse for that session.

The session plans include a suggestion on how to teach the weekly verse to a large group in a way that is both fun and effective. It will help the kids better understand the meaning of the verse as well as how to apply it. You will also find suggestions for adapting these activities to teach the younger children (grades K–2) a shortened version of the verse. If you have room in your Bible story area, you can have the older children and the younger children move to opposite sides of the room so they can work on their verses without bothering each other. If not, consider dismissing the children in grades K–2 earlier than the older kids so that they can work on their verses at their small group sites.

 ## Life Application

The Overview

For your convenience, an overview box is printed at the top of the Life Application Page in each session. It is intended to give you a quick picture of the On-the-Job Training Topic, Action Step, Bible story basis, memory verse, and a list of things you'll need to accomplish during your small group time. Here's a sample:

Materials

A reproducible Life Application Page for small group leaders is included in this curriculum at the end of the instructions for each weekly session. (See the first weekly page on p. 59.) The Life Application Pages are intended to provide small group leaders with the information they need to conduct successful group times. The pages include questions to ask the kids, explanations of On-the-Job Training Topics, prayer reminders, Action Step chal-

---

ON-THE-JOB TRAINING TOPIC:
Care for each other in God's family

ACTION STEP:
Listen to others the way Jesus would

BIBLE STORY:
Acts 2:42–47; Acts 4:32–35

MEMORY VERSE:
1 John 4:11 (NIV)

THINGS YOU'LL NEED:

- Copy of "Tips for Small Group Leaders" from pages 23–24
- Action Step/Training Topic poster (made in advance)
- Children's Journal

- Adventure Prayer poster (made in advance)
- Children's Activity Book
- Newsprint
- Marker
- Chalkboard and chalk

IN ADVANCE:
Make a tool-shaped poster of the Adventure Prayer on page 24. Also make tool-shaped posters of the Action Step and On-the-Job Training Topic.

Setup

The Life Application section, which comes after the Bible story presentation, may be done during the middle portion or at the end of each session.

During this time the children are encouraged to draw a connection between the message of the Bible story and its application to their lives. A small group led by a friendly, caring adult makes it easier for shy or quiet children to risk sharing their private thoughts and feelings. This activity is best done in small groups (in their own special place) where the kids can feel comfortable enough to reflect on and discuss what they have learned.

lenges, and tips to make the small group time more effective. You will need to make copies of these pages to give to the small group leaders. You will need to distribute each Life Application Page at least one week ahead of time so that the small group leaders will be able to prepare for the sessions at home.

Each group leader will also need to make a poster of the Adventure Prayer and posters of the weekly Action Steps and On-the-Job Training Topics. These posters could be made in the shape of tools (a hammer, wrench, or screwdriver) to add to the overall construction theme. (For additional details, see the section "Tips for Small Group Leaders" on p. 23.)

ADDITIONAL MATERIAL FOR CHILDREN'S CHURCH WORSHIP AND MIDWEEK CLUB

If you are using this curriculum for Children's Church or a Midweek Club, these are the extra session components we have provided for you.

 ## Children's Church Worship

The extra components included for this option are:

Singing

Songs based on the Bible memory verses are included in this curriculum beginning on page 119. The same songs by Christine Wyrtzen are included on a sing-along cassette, *Bible Memory Toolbox.* To order copies of the tape, see page 128. If time allows, you may also want to include a few familiar songs that relate to the weekly On-the-Job Training Topics. If your children's music collection needs a bit of updating, check out what's new at your local Christian bookstore. We suggest looking at works by Mary Rice Hopkins and Rob Evans, "The Donut Man."

Critter County Story

The children who have been on a 50-Day Adventure in past years will be familiar with the Critter County characters. Other children may also know them through the popular children's music tapes based on Critter County. Although these stories (based on the weekly themes and Action Steps) are aimed at early elementary aged children, their brevity and humor make older children fans, too. Through the stories the children will see the critters face situations in which they learn how to do their part to make the church all God wants it to be.

Offering Time

Scripture calls the practice of bringing God monetary offerings an act of worship. You may want to give the kids a chance to worship God in this manner; if you do, consider doing something more than just asking the kids to place their money in a collection plate or basket. Encourage them to thank God out loud for one of his blessings each time they place an offering in the basket, or to bring a food item for your local food pantry. (Children who don't have a monetary offering to give can still take part by thanking God for something when the offering basket passes by them.)

Praise and Prayer

The praise and prayer suggestions are intended to give children the opportunity to praise God as a group. You will find a variety of prayer ideas suggested to help kids learn how to pray and to help them feel comfortable praying aloud.

 **Midweek Extras**

The extra components for this option are:

Game

Games are an important tool in teaching kids how to cooperate and follow directions, and it's hard to beat a good game for its entertainment value. Also, a well constructed game can help reinforce the point of a lesson. But we know, as you do, that few games are equally good for all ages, all settings, and all time frames. That's why we offer suggestions on how to adapt the games to different situations. Some of the game suggestions are of the non-competitive variety. They encourage physical activity and fun without creating winners and losers. Of course, you can choose to substitute game ideas of your own if you so desire. You know best what will work in your setting.

It would be wise to use a permission slip for the games section. See page 127 for a sample.

Critter County Story

After an active game, let your kids cool off in Critter County, where something interesting is always taking place. Children who have been on a 50-Day Adventure before will be familiar with the Critter County characters, and they'll enjoy helping their friends get to know them, too. Each week's tale is based on the weekly theme or Action Step. These brief stories are written with early elementary children in mind, but the older children can benefit from them, too. These charming critters have a way of capturing everybody's interest while

helping children discover their part in making the church a place where all feel they belong.

Singing

You can reinforce the memory verses and Adventure topics by teaching the songs included in this book, beginning on page 119. A sing-along cassette tape of this music, *Bible Memory Toolbox*, is also available. To order copies of the tape, see page 128. You will probably also want to use a few songs the children already know. Help the children learn to view group singing as a pleasant time of celebration and worship.

HOW CAN THE MATERIALS BE ADAPTED FOR USE IN SMALL AND LARGE CHURCHES?

The material in this curriculum may be used by an individual teacher with a small class or by a team of several teachers with lots of kids. Whether your church is of the small, medium, or large variety, the 50-Day Adventure can work for you. The following tips will help you adapt the material to your setting.

Small Churches

Small churches usually face the twin challenges of limited staff and limited space when planning special programs for kids, but challenges can be overcome with ingenuity. Look over the list of Bible-time projects that would work best in your situation. Think of people in your church who might enjoy helping kids with a woodworking, sewing, or cooking project. If limited space is a factor for you, offer only two or three project options at a time. Then when the kids complete them, you can introduce two or three new ones. Choose projects that you will be able to store easily from week to week.

The ideal staffing for three project sites is three adults, but one or two individuals can successfully supervise three projects if the number of children is small and there are older kids in the group to lend the younger ones a helping hand. The nice thing about the suggested Bible-time projects for this Adventure is that they don't all require step-by-step instructions. The main role of the adult is to help kids discover what life was like in Bible times.

The same adult doesn't have to oversee the same project each week, but it's easier that way. It's also nice for the kids to work with adults who know them. If you are able to find only one or two individuals willing to supervise the projects, see if you can find someone to help at least with setup and cleanup each week. Having more than one project supervisor on hand at a time helps when a substitute is needed. People are more willing to step in at the last minute to help if there is someone with experience on hand to answer their questions. Note that certain projects require direct adult supervision. You will need to plan your staffing accordingly.

Combining the children into one group for Bible Story Time will reduce the number of people needed to present the weekly dramas. Senior citizens and teens just might love the opportunity to put their acting skills to use. If necessary, revise the scripts so that they can be read as stories.

For Life Application Time, your entire group of kids might be small enough to be their own small group. But even if you have 10 kids, you might want to divide into two smaller groups. You will need one committed Christian adult for every small group, because one of the goals of Life Application Time is to develop a relationship between the kids and a caring Christian role model.

If you are using the curriculum for one class only you might consider these suggestions: Choose one or two projects for kids to work on at the start of each class. For story time you could copy the provided scripts onto cards and let kids help you do the stories by reading the various parts. Then you could keep your class all together for Life Application Time.

Large Churches

Large churches not only have a bigger talent pool to draw from for staffing, they also have more children to work with. The challenge for large churches can be one of commitment. In the large church, the sense of being needed is diminished by assuming there is someone else around to do the job. People look for short-term, convenient assignments because they know there are lots of other people available to lend a hand.

This 50-Day Adventure for kids allows you to subdivide the duties in many ways. Individuals can commit to working on one activity or project each week, or to working just a couple of weeks. Different people will be attracted to the dramas, creative projects, music, games, and record-keeping activities. But there are two positions that need to be filled by people willing to make an eight-week commitment—the coordinator and the small group leaders. One of the goals of Life Application is to develop a relationship between the kids and a caring Christian role model, someone with whom they'll become comfortable enough to share their thoughts and feelings, and to partner with in prayer.

This won't happen if a new face shows up each week in the role of the small group leader. Ask God to help you find the people he has equipped for this task. If you show them how much they are needed, an eight-week commitment should be no problem.

Tips for Small Group Leaders

For Life Application

(See p. 25 for photocopy permission.)

Life Application Time provides the children and you a chance to retreat to a quiet place to talk and pray together. Small groups should have between six and eight children in them. The children you are assigned on the first day will remain in your group during the whole Adventure. This means that it is important for you to commit to taking part in each week's session. The two main goals of your small group time are as follows:

1. To help the children apply truths from the Bible story that will guide them in making decisions about their relationship with Jesus and his church.

2. To help the children develop faith-building relationships with a Christian adult (you) and with a group of Christian peers (the other kids in your group).

You will be given a "Life Application Page for Small Group Leaders" for each of the eight weekly Adventure sessions. These pages include information to help you accomplish the Small Group Time goals. Each page has two main sections:

KID TALK

This section provides questions for leaders to ask to begin a guided discussion. These are open-ended questions that encourage children to think and talk about how to apply the Bible lesson to their lives. This is not a time to retell the Bible story or to tell the kids what the point of the lesson is. Think of your role as

leading the children to the discovery of insights rather than dispensing knowledge.

The Kid Talk section is also a time to discuss the weekly Adventure On-the-Job Training Topics and Action Steps. To help your kids review the Training Topics and Action Steps, write or paint each one on a piece of poster board. Having the poster board cut out in the shape of a tool will add to the overall construction theme of the Adventure.

PRAYER TALK

This section gives you and the children the opportunity to develop an interest in praying as a group and praying for each other. Begin by making a poster of the Adventure Prayer that fits your age-group. (See p. 24.) Then use the prayer each week. Also remember to ask the kids if they have any prayer requests. (It often helps them open up if you share a concern of your own and ask them to pray for you.) As they get to know you and each other better, you can encourage them to take turns praying short sentence prayers.

THE ADVENTURE PRAYER FOR GRADES K–2

Dear Jesus,

I want to be part of a caring church family. Show me how to make (name of friend) feel loved and welcomed.

Amen.

THE ADVENTURE PRAYER FOR GRADES 3–6

Dear Jesus,

I want to be part of a caring church family. Teach me to listen to others the way you do. Show me how to make (name of friend) feel loved and welcomed.

Amen.

Photocopy Permission

"TO PHOTOCOPY OR NOT TO PHOTOCOPY?" . . . THAT IS THE QUESTION!

All portions of this curriculum are copyright protected and may not be reproduced in any form, *unless otherwise indicated*, without written permission of The Chapel Ministries.

The following pages may be photocopied and distributed to the appropriate children's Adventure staff members without written permission. Please note and honor the stated restrictions. This permission is granted with the understanding that the copied pages be used solely for the 50-Day Adventure, and that they will be destroyed at the end of the program. This permission is granted to the purchaser only and may not be transferred to another individual or organization.

PHOTOCOPY PERMISSION

The Big Picture (pgs. 5–9) . . . . .1 copy per staff member

**Ready to Begin—
Administrative Information (pgs. 11–14)** . . . . .1 copy per staff member

**Ready to Begin—
Weekly Leader Information (pgs. 15–22)** . . . . .1 copy per staff member

Tips for Small Group Leaders (pgs. 23–24) . . . . .1 copy per small group leader

Bible-Time Projects (pgs. 27–49) . . . . .1 copy per planner and project leader

Bible Story Time . . . . .1 copy per leader, performer, and
(pages from weekly sessions) small group leader

Children's Church Worship . . . . .1 copy per worship and song leader
(pages from weekly sessions) and story reader

Midweek Extras . . . . .1 copy per game leader, song leader,
(pages from weekly sessions) and story reader

Life Application Time . . . . .1 copy per small group leader
(pages from weekly sessions)

Adventure Songs (pgs. 119–122) . . . . .1 copy per song leader and
accompanist

Evaluation Form (pgs. 123–124) . . . . .As needed

Cube Pattern (p. 125) . . . . .1 copy per child

Sample Project and Activity Permission Slip (p. 127). . .As needed

Order Form (p. 128) . . . . .As needed

 # Bible-Time Projects

(See p. 25 for photocopy permission.)

WHAT ARE BIBLE-TIME PROJECTS?

Bible-time projects are learning experiences that take participants back to Bible days. Bible accounts become more than just stories as kids begin to get a feel for how the people of the Bible lived. What they ate, what they wore, what their homes were like, are all topics the kids are given the opportunity to explore through hands-on activities. At each site children are encouraged to research a specific topic and then work collectively to complete a project that demonstrates what they've learned. Because figuring out how to make the projects is part of the learning experience, there are some projects that will not have step-by-step instructions. This gives the kids a richer learning experience and more ownership of what they create. The adult leaders working in the Bible-time project areas supervise and guide, rather than direct, the activities. The leaders also help the children understand how each project relates to life during Bible times.

HOW DO BIBLE-TIME PROJECTS WORK?

• Bible-time project work sites are set up to accommodate 10 to 12 kids each, with one leader for each site.

• During each session, kids choose their own project sites and decide how long to work at each one. (A child may choose to spend 10 minutes at one project area and then join a different project.) Some kids will choose to work at the same site for all eight weeks, whereas others may opt to rotate to a number of different sites from week to week. Some of the projects offered in this section can be done in one or two weeks' time, while others may take the full eight weeks to complete. Kids in grades K–6 will intermingle with one another, each contributing to the projects according to his or her developmental level.

• It is the site leader's responsibility to provide his or her site with suitable reference materials and supplies to complete the project. As kids arrive, they must research the project to figure out how to use the supplies to complete it. Suggestions for reference materials are included on page 28.

• New project sites can be added as the children complete or lose interest in old ones. Some project sites will be more appropriate to certain sessions than others. Certain projects require consistency among workers if the aim is a group presentation of some sort.

• On the first day of the Adventure, the children should be given a quick look at each of the projects and allowed to choose the one they want to work on first.

• If you have chosen to run the Adventure in a more traditional Sunday school setting— one teacher, one class, one room—just pick one or two projects appropriate for your group to do each week.

HOW MUCH WORK IS THIS GOING TO BE?

It is important to note that you have control over how complicated or simple you want to make each of the Bible-time projects and how elaborately you choose to furnish the area. The suggested projects are just that—suggestions. Feel free to simplify, replace, or develop projects with ideas of your own.

The hardest part of Bible-time projects is done before the Adventure begins. Once you have selected the projects and gathered the resources, the majority of your time is spent overseeing the setup from week to week. Don't be shy about asking people for help when you need it. The most successful programs are usually the result of team efforts rather than solo performances.

HOW DO I GET ORGANIZED?

Start with a brainstorming and planning session with all of your leaders and adult helpers to decide which projects would work best for your group. Have this meeting six to eight weeks before the Adventure begins. Try answering questions such as:

- How many projects will we need? (A good rule of thumb is one project for every 10 to 12 kids.)
- Which projects would our kids enjoy the most?
- How much space is available for project sites?
- What are the strongest interests and talents among our project leaders?
- What project resources are readily available?
- What projects work best within the budget?
- How will we set up and decorate each project site area?
- How can the projects be stored?

WHERE CAN I FIND RESOURCES?

The next step is to obtain the resource materials you will need to help students research the projects. Look for these in your church library, educational resource room, Christian or general bookstore, or ask your pastor to loan you his or her personal reference materials. There are additional suggestions under specific project descriptions. Resource materials may include:

- Bible dictionaries
- Bible encyclopedias

- Bible atlases
- Picture Bibles
- Christian books
- Bible cookbooks
- Study Bibles

Here are the titles of some books you may be able to find at your Christian bookstore:

Growing Up in Bible Times by Margaret Embry, Published by Thomas Nelson Publishers, © 1995

Everyday Life in Bible Times by Margaret Embry, Published by Thomas Nelson Publishers, © 1995

The Complete Family Guide to Jewish Holidays by Dalia Hardof Renberg, Published by Adama Books, © 1985

The Picture Bible by Iva Hoth, Published by Chariot Books, © 1978

Bible Times Crafts for Kids by Neva Hickerson, Published by Gospel Light, © 1993

Christian Crafts from Milk Containers by Joanne Hooker, Published by Shining Star Publications, © 1994

Christian Crafts from Nature's Gifts by Anita Reith Stohs, Published by Shining Star Publications, © 1994

The Children's Illustrated Bible by Selina Hastings, Published by Dorling Kindersley, Inc., © 1994

While they are not mentioned in the supply list for each project, you will want to have resources like these available. But be sure to keep them in a safe place. After you have researched your projects you will need to obtain the necessary supplies needed to complete each one. After a thorough search of your own supply room, think about borrowing items from church members and other local churches. You can publicize your needs in a church bulletin, newsletter, bulletin board, or by sending a letter home to parents or all members of the congregation. If you still come up short on project supplies, try these:

- Craft store
- Hardware store
- Christian bookstore
- Art supply store
- School supply store
- Old Sunday school art

Be careful to include all supplies needed to accomplish your goal. Give thought to measuring, cutting, pasting, and writing tools before you begin. Make sure that everything you need is available for the kids when they arrive.

WHAT DO I NEED TO KNOW ABOUT SETTING UP THE PROJECT SITES?

Exercise care and caution when assigning site areas for each project. Give consideration to:

- The amount of space needed to complete the project
- The noise level involved in construction or rehearsal of a project
- The mess factor involved in the project

(Projects requiring water, hand washing, or other special needs should be located near water access areas.)

Project sites can be flexible according to your church's available space. If you have one large room you can use for both the Bible-time projects and the Bible story, you could put each project on tables that can be moved around as needed. Projects too large for tables could be done on the floor. If you have several smaller classrooms, you could put one or two projects in each room. Just make sure the kids know where all the projects are so they can find them easily. Projects can even be

worked on in a hallway (on tables) as long as people meeting in nearby rooms can close the doors to keep out the chatter of enthusiastic workers! Decorating the project sites is optional. Consult Bible dictionaries, encyclopedias, or picture Bibles for ideas on how to give your sites a thematic effect.

WHO DOES CLEANUP?

Allow for several minutes at the end of each project time to clean up. The project leader should give direction as to what is expected. Kids may collect supplies, pick up scraps, and clean up the area.

If your time frame is tight and there's not an extra five minutes for cleanup, the kids could do a minimal straightening and the adult at the project area could put things away while the kids are at Bible Story Time or while they leave to go home.

WHERE DO I STORE THE PROJECTS?

How you store the projects will depend on their type and size. Paper projects might be rolled up, stacked, kept in a file folder, or placed in a box. Small three-dimensional projects might be kept in boxes or on a cabinet shelf. Large projects might be placed on top of a file cabinet or storage cabinet or locked in a storage room. Label each project for easy reference, and include a sign that says "Please don't touch! This is a 50-Day Adventure project!"

HOW CAN I HAVE SUCCESSFUL PROJECTS?

- The best learning experiences happen when participants take part in, discover, think, handle, and question. Leaders need to encourage the kids to experiment, create, and seek their own answers at every stage of a project.

• Leaders need to be sure kids understand how the projects relate to Bible times or the 50-Day Adventure. Leaders can do this by encouraging the children to research their projects and to discuss their impressions and opinions as they work, and by asking questions such as, "How would you like to live in a place like this?" "What would you compare this flavor to?" or "Why do you think they wore clothes that looked like this?"

• Each child will have his or her own personal abilities. Leaders should provide as much help as the children need—but no more. Rather than "teach," leaders should encourage kids to discover and experience. Leaders need to help kids discover where their strengths lie.

• To be sure all the leaders understand the big picture of the G. H. Construction Crew Adventure and grasp how the Bible-time projects fit in, give each leader a copy of the sections "The Big Picture" and "Bible-Time Projects."

• Have the projects set up and ready to begin about 20 minutes before the start of class. As soon as the children arrive, they can begin to work. This option works even if you choose to offer the Bible-time projects as the last portion of your session.

• The first week or two the kids will need plenty of guidance to understand this new approach. The leaders need to keep reinforcing the idea that the kids can try any project they like and even switch projects if they choose.

• It's helpful to have basic instruction posters taped to the table or wall at each project area. That way the kids can take more initiative for figuring out what to do. In particular, provide written directions for projects that involve measuring, mixing, researching, and building.

▶ BIBLE-TIME PROJECTS ◀

Use these suggestions, or think of your own creative ideas!

Be sure to have adult supervision where noted. Also, it may be wise to make a sample of the more complex projects before doing them with kids. This will enable you to discover the best way to help kids with the projects. But because you want the kids to use their own creativity, please refrain from showing your samples until children have finished their projects.

1. BIBLE-TIME DRAMA PROJECT

Goal: Children will prepare a drama based on the story of Paul's vision of the man of Macedonia, and Lydia's conversion in Philippi. This will be presented as the Bible Story Time drama in Week 6. Students will be encouraged to put together this drama to present as an example of taking care of the world and its people.

Length: This project will require the same participants each week so that they can plan, prepare, and practice for their performance in Week 6. The students will need to decide how extensive they wish their drama to be, and how involved they want to get with set design, costumes, scriptwriting, and memorization. This project will take at least five weeks to develop.

Supplies: Bible-time costumes for all characters (including Roman soldiers) and props as noted in the suggestions that follow.

Directions: Begin by reading Acts 16:6–15 with the group. Let children suggest ways to act out what the story is communicating. Remind them that Week 6's Training Topic is "Help in other places" and the Action Step is "Take care of the world and its people." If the kids need guidance (or if you aren't using this as a project but still need a skit for the Week 6 Bible Story Presentation), you might use the following suggestions.

Guidelines for Drama:

1. Students must settle on a drama style that everyone is comfortable with.

• Will the action take place precisely as told in the Bible?
• Will the story be told by "witnesses" to the action?
• Will it be an interview with the main characters in the story?
• Do you want to present a contemporary drama reflecting back on the Bible story?

2. Students must decide what scenes will be necessary. Here are some suggested scenes to work with:

Act 1: Paul's Vision/Acts 16:6–10

Scene A: Introduction—The characters could give some background on Paul's previous ministry. You can acquire this information by reading the opening summary of the Book of Acts found in many Bibles. Show a map of Paul's previous travels. Tell the characters to speak to the audience as if they were the crowds that gathered to hear Paul speak. You may wish to incorporate your Bible-Time Wardrobe Roman Soldier Project in this drama; this scene can provide you the opportunity to have Roman soldiers standing guard over the audience as they listen to Paul teach about Jesus.

Scene B: Have characters portray Paul's vision of the man of Macedonia. Emphasize that there are people all over the world who need to hear about Jesus. You may wish to conclude your scene by reminding kids how God wants us all to reach out to others by providing food and clothes for those who need them and by sharing his Word. (It is assumed that at this point in Scripture the disciple Luke, the author of Acts, joined Paul in his ministry at Troas.)

Act 2: Lydia's Conversion/ Acts 16:11–15

Scene A: Have characters begin with Paul's journey out to sea, heading toward Philippi. This would be an excellent opportunity to use a boat as a prop.

Scene B: As Luke and Paul gather in Philippi on the Sabbath to pray, they discover several women, one of whom is Lydia. Illustrate Lydia's family becoming Christians and being baptized. In closing, as Lydia invites Paul and Luke to stay at her house, draw the conclusion that it is still our responsibility to care for others in times of need today.

3. Students must decide what characters are needed.

• A great deal will depend on how many students want to be involved in this project. If you have a large number of children to work with, you will need crowds to witness the action or respond to the story.
• When selecting main characters, be certain students understand the responsibility involved in taking a lead role. Large parts require more work.
• Recommended characters include:

Act 1: Paul, Luke, and companions (as many as needed based on the number of students), and the man of Macedonia.

Act 2: Paul, Luke, companions, Lydia, her family, and women (as many as you need based on the number of students).

4. Students must decide what props are needed. Painted backgrounds are suggested as a separate project on page 49. Here are suggestions for other props:

Act 1

Scene A: Spears for Roman soldiers and a large Bible-time map showing some of the places to which Paul has traveled.

Scene B: A wooden table, a chair, and what looks like a bedroll on the floor. This will help give the audience the impression that Paul is in a Bible-time home.

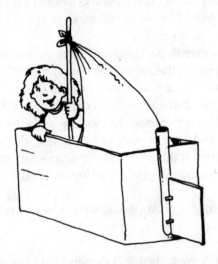

Act 2

Scene A: This scene takes place in a boat out at sea. Kids may wish to construct a cardboard boat for realistic action and fun. (Making props is an excellent way to include in drama children who don't feel comfortable with on-stage roles.) If your manpower or supplies are limited, write into your script descriptive remarks that characters can make come alive as they pantomime motions to present the drama.

Scene B: Same as Act 1, Scene B

Questions: To help the kids figure out a good way to present the drama or to help them understand it as they develop and practice it, ask questions like these: How do you think Paul and his companions felt traveling around, spreading God's Word? Remind students that not everyone was anxious to hear God's message, and that at times, preaching God's Word was a very dangerous vocation. Can you think of some countries where this is still true today? How do you think Paul felt when he saw his vision? In what ways do we receive messages from God today? What are some things we can do to help others, especially people in different countries? What exciting thing happened to Lydia? How do you think she felt?

2. BIBLE-TIME WARDROBE PROJECT

Goal: Participants will research and design two types of Bible-time apparel. Use this project to provide costumes for your Bible-Time Drama Project.

Length: This project can take anywhere from one to several weeks to complete.

Supplies: Pictures of Roman soldiers and Bible-time people, fabric remnants (solids and stripes work best), ribbons, measuring tapes, scissors, vinyl fabric, Velcro, glue, poster board, silver and gold trims, silver spray paint or aluminum foil, and needles and thread or a sewing machine (sewing items are optional)

In Advance: Obtain fabric remnants by asking for donations or by browsing the discount piles in a fabric store.

Directions: Provide as many pictures of clothing worn during Bible times as you can find. Try to supply kids with illustrations of both Jewish tunics and headpieces,

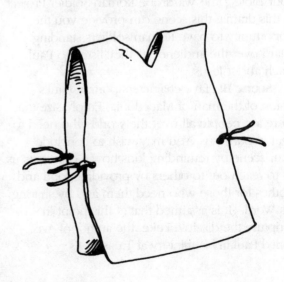

as well as an ensemble of Roman soldier costumes. Because the children will be using scissors and sewing, you will need to have an adult or older teen working with this group.

Tunics can be made with a strip of fabric twice the length of a child's torso. Cut holes in the center of the fabric for children to put their heads through. Decorate tunics with silver and gold trims. Then cut holes on each side for attaching ribbon for kids to tie. (See illustration on previous page.) Older children may wish to stitch up the sides by hand or with a machine. A guide for cutting a child's tunic would be to make it 14" wide from shoulder to shoulder. Make the neck cutout a 5" (down) V-neck. The length of the tunic should be about 25" to make it knee length. For an adult tunic: 18" wide from shoulder to shoulder; 8" (down) V-neck; and 40" long. These measurements will need to be adjusted for individual children and adults. Use fabric for belts.

Headpieces require plain, light-colored fabric squares. Tie the headpiece around the top of the head by using a length of fabric to fasten the material over the forehead area (shepherd style). Another way to fashion a headpiece is to place the material on the head like a shawl, flipping the longer end under the chin and over the shoulder.

Roman Soldier costumes can be made by providing participants with a variety of materials and letting them use their imaginations. Start by cutting out vests (front and back with shoulders on the fold) and skirts (front only) from sturdy material, such as vinyl (an adult will need to help with this). Then punch holes in the two lower corners of the vest, for tying the vest on, or you may want to attach Velcro. Cut holes along the top of the skirt for tying on a belt that will hold the skirt in place. Again, you may wish to attach the belt with Velcro. Next, use the lighter-weight fabric for cutting out vest bars and skirt petals. Kids will attach these by gluing. Here are some measurements to help you:

Child's Vest:	4" shoulder pieces (length and width); 12" length (for torso); and 12" width
Child's Skirt:	13" waist; 12" length; and 15" width across the bottom
Adult Vest:	6" shoulder pieces (length and width); 19" length (for torso); and 18" width
Adult Skirt:	19" waist; 20" length; and 22" width across the bottom

Vest bars for child and adult are about 1-1/2" x 6"–9"

Skirt petals for child and adult are about 3" x 4"

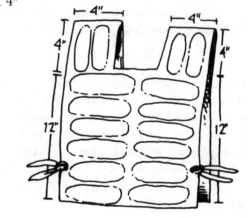

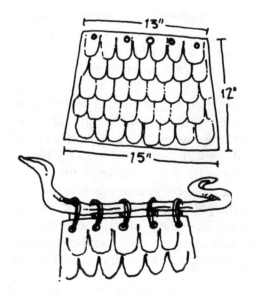

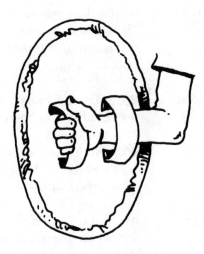

Children can make shields by using poster board. Cut it into a circular shape. Cut hand-holds as shown, and cover with aluminum foil or spray paint. Children may also want to decorate their shields with the gold and silver trim items.

Questions: As students work on costumes, ask questions like these: Why did Jewish people and Roman soldiers dress so differently? Why do you think tunics were a popular dress for Jewish people? Why don't we use tunics today? What restrictions may have been placed on people using this type of clothing? What were the benefits?

Optional Kindergarten Supplies: Bible storybooks, cutout Bible-time clothing items (which leaders will need to make in advance), crayons and markers, and paper dolls

Kindergarten Suggestion: Let children page through Bible storybooks to see the different types of clothes worn during Bible times. Provide them with cutout pictures of Bible-time clothing. Have them decorate the clothes by drawing multi-colored stripes in tunics, or coloring the petals of soldier skirts. When they are finished, have them cut out the clothes and try them on paper dolls. Let the children create dialogue as their paper doll tells others about Jesus.

3. BIBLE-TIME CARPENTRY PROJECT

You will need to have adults or older teens helping with each of these projects. It would be wise to make samples ahead of time. Because of the potential risk involved with the saw project, it is suggested that it be offered to older children only and that an adult skilled in building and use of a saw be supervising. Also, most of the supplies for these projects will need to be purchased from a hardware store.

Goal: The kids will make a Bible-time measuring stick, hammer, and saw. These were tools of Jesus' time. Use this project to help the kids understand the difference between carpentry tools today and the tools in Bible times. The tools can be shown by the leader in Week 4 to talk about using our tools well.

Length: You may wish to offer this project for several weeks, and work on a different tool each week. Each of the three tools can be completed in one week.

Measuring Stick Supplies (per child): Two pieces of 1/8" thick, smooth, wood cut 6-1/2" long and 1" wide with one hole drilled near the end of each piece; heavy duty string; sandpaper; permanent marker; ruler; and a pair of disposable latex gloves (can be purchased at a drug store)

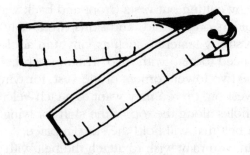

Directions: Allow kids to look through the Bible resource books you have provided. Help them discover facts such as: Carpentry has been an occupation since at least 2000

B.C. Carpenters constructed boats, domestic articles, and farm tools. They used wood, metal, and stone. Wooden parts were joined together by simple nails or wood dowels.

Encourage children to make the measuring stick first, so that it can be used to create the hammer and saw. To make the sticks, have kids sand the edges of the two wood pieces. Then tie them together loosely enough so that the measuring stick can be opened into a straight line. Using a ruler, make inch marks on the stick with the permanent markers. (Make sure kids put on disposable gloves before doing this part to keep from permanently marking their hands.) Leave the measuring sticks flat to dry, then fold.

Hammer Supplies (per child): One 7" long dowel 1/2" thick (for the handle), a block of hardwood 1-1/2" x 3" by 1" thick for the head (with a hole drilled in the underside 3/4" deep for inserting the dowel), sandpaper, wood glue (available at a hardware store), and damp cleanup rags

Optional Supplies: Scrap lumber (a soft wood like pine, for example), pencils, nails, and colored string

Directions: Hand children the wood pieces to sand. Have them sand both pieces until they are smooth. Then have kids attach the hammer head to the handle by first filling the hole in the hammer head with glue and then inserting the dowel into the hole. Wipe off excess glue with a damp rag. Set hammers on their heads to dry. Let them dry for at least

one week. In subsequent weeks you may wish to provide the optional supplies listed to allow children an opportunity to experiment with their hammers. Challenge them to create a simple symbol of the times by drawing dots approximately one inch apart on the scrap lumber. Instruct participants to exercise care when using hammers as they pound nails into positions marked by the dots. Use colored string to loop around the nails to complete the design.

Saw Supplies (per child): 6 pieces of wood (Top piece 4-1/2" x 3/4"; middle piece 5-1/2" x 3/4"; 4 side pieces 3" x 3/4" each), Coping saw blade (similar to a hacksaw) 6-1/2" long, 12 metal washers, 6 screws (1/4" diameter and 2-1/2" long), and 6 wing nuts

In Advance: Drill holes for screws as shown in illustration. Holes should be about 5/16" diameter. Make sure the holes are spaced to line up with the holes in the blade.

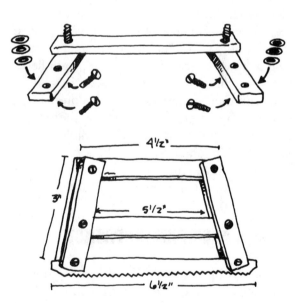

Directions: First lay top piece, two side pieces, and middle piece on work area. Insert screws so that they are pointing up. (See illustration.) Place three washers on each screw that will be holding the blade, then add the blade. Next, add three more washers onto the

back of the blade (which is facing up). Lay second set of side pieces on top. Add wing nuts to each of the screws and tighten screws until saw blade is secure and saw handles are sturdy.

Questions: As the students make their tools, the leader of the project could ask questions like these: How do Bible-time tools differ from the tools used today? How are they alike? How would workers in Bible times be limited as to what they could do? Who are some Bible-time carpenters you may have read or heard about?

Optional Kindergarten Supplies: Modern-day hammer, a sturdy piece of wood with pre-drilled holes, and dowels to fit in the holes

Kindergarten Suggestion: Both the measuring stick and hammer can be made by younger children. After they have created a measuring stick, let them experiment with measuring items around the project site. Ask them what kinds of measuring tools they have seen their parents use at home. If you choose to let younger children make hammers, provide a sturdy piece of wood with pre-drilled holes for children to hammer small dowels into with their hammers. Show children a modern day hammer and then ask them to identify the "missing" part of the Bible-time hammer. Encourage them to think of creative ways Bible-time carpenters may have removed nails that were hammered in by mistake!

4. MUSICAL INSTRUMENT PROJECT

Goal: Children will have the opportunity to create several different instruments similar to those used during Bible times. In doing so, they can compare Bible-time music to today's music. Tell students that instruments were used to provide music during temple services, to summon people together for meetings, and to signal occasions of danger or celebration.

Use this project to remind students that music is also an expression of praise to the Lord. Suggested instruments to make are string harps, tambourines, and rattles. This project fits in particularly well with Weeks 4, 7, and 8. Week 7 would be a great time for kids to use their instruments during a praise time.

Length: This project can take one or more weeks, depending on the variety of instrument-making offered.

Harp Supplies (per child): 3/4" plastic tubing cut into a 15" length, 6 pieces of 13" fish line (20 or 30 lb.), a sharp instrument to poke holes in the tubing for the fish line to attach, blunt-edged needles, and scissors

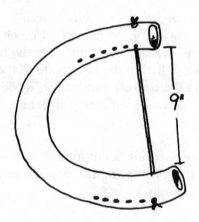

Directions: Bend the tubing so that it is in the shape of a C. To help it hold its shape, thread the longest piece of fish line through the top and bottom holes using a needle. (An adult or older teen should supervise and remind children to be careful so they do not

stick their fingers with the needles.) Pull the fishing line tight enough to make the distance between the top and the bottom of the C nine inches. Tie knots to hold the fishing line in place at both ends and cut off excess fishing line. Continue to attach other lines the same way. Tighten each line to a different tautness to create a variety of sounds.

Tambourine Supplies (per child): Sturdy paper or plastic plates, glue, paper punch, small pebbles or beans, yarn, beads, and other decorating items

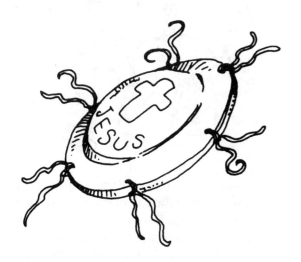

In Advance: Punch 6 evenly spaced holes around the edges of each set of plates.

Directions: Have kids decorate the bottoms of plates. Then place beans or pebbles onto one plate. Add a line of glue around the edge of this plate. Put the second plate on top. Make sure the two plates are securely fastened with the glue. Then add yarn streamers, tying them through the holes. Allow the tambourines to dry for at least one week before using.

Rattle Supplies (per child): A pop can, 6" long dowel (no thicker than 5/8"), dried peas, duct tape, scissors, and clay

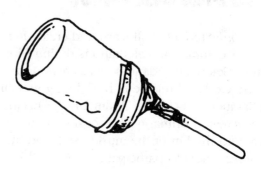

Directions: Have children fill cans about 1/4 full of peas. Insert dowel into mouth of can and secure with clay. Then tape with duct tape to make sure the dowel stays attached to the can.

Questions: Encourage kids to talk about their favorite kinds of music and how music has changed through the ages. Use questions like these: What are the similarities and differences in Bible-time music and music today? For what occasions were instruments used during Bible times? (Celebrations, worship, and to signal danger) For what occasions are instruments used today? Who are some Bible-time musicians? What musicians do you admire today? How are they similar to or different from Bible-time musicians?

Optional Kindergarten Supplies: Bible Memory Toolbox sing-along cassette or other Bible song cassettes, and a cassette player

Kindergarten Suggestion: Tambourines and rattles would probably work the best with this age-group. After kids complete the instruments, let children use them while singing or listening to Bible songs or the *Bible Memory Toolbox* sing-along cassette by Christine Wyrtzen. Encourage them to march, stomp, and parade as they celebrate God's messages with music!

5. BIBLE-TIME DANCE PROJECT

Goal: Students will learn and create folk dances common in celebrations during Bible times. Celebratory dances were created to praise God and rejoice in him during worship. (2 Samuel 6:14–15 and Psalm 149:2–3) Dances were created primarily by focusing on the beat and rhythm of the music used, and by inviting others to participate in moves that were simple and repetitious. Groups often danced in circles to symbolize unity and care for others in God's family. You may wish to have the group present a celebratory worship dance in Week 7 or 8.

Length: This project will take one to four weeks. It will depend on how involved children wish to get, and if you are preparing for a larger performance.

Supplies: Cassette of Israeli music (available at the library) and a cassette player

Directions: The Hora is a popular Jewish folk dance. The Hora begins slowly and speeds up gradually with the rhythm of the music. Dance the Hora in a large circle, arms on each other's shoulders, and facing the inside of the circle.

On the 1st beat:	Take a step to the right with the right foot.
On the 2nd beat:	Cross the left foot behind the right.
On the 3rd beat:	Take another step to the right with the right foot.
On the 4th beat:	Cross the left foot in front of the right foot and kick with the left foot.
On the 5th beat:	Take a step to the left with the left foot.
On the 6th beat:	Cross the right foot behind the left.
On the 7th beat:	Take another step to the left with the left foot.
On the 8th beat:	Cross the right foot in front of the left foot and kick with the right foot.

Repeat all eight steps.

For variation, encourage the kids to think of their own steps! Remember to keep the movements simple and repetitive.

Questions: As students listen to music and attempt to put together a celebratory dance, ask these questions: Why do you think people danced in worship to the Lord? How is movement an expression of praise? How do today's dances differ from the worship dances of the past?

Kindergarten Suggestion: Little ones may do a simplified Hora:

On the 1st beat:	Take a step to the right with the right foot.
On the 2nd beat:	Kick the left foot in front of the right.
On the 3rd beat:	Take a step to the left with the left foot.
On the 4th beat:	Kick the right foot in front of the left.

Repeat all four steps.

Encourage children to think of simple ways to move, and let others follow the examples given.

6. POTTERY-MAKING PROJECT

Goal: Pottery served a number of different purposes during Bible times. It was molded to create a variety of utensils, containers, and ornate items for wealthier families. Encourage the children to research how pottery was developed by looking in Bible dictionaries and art books. Clay combined with fine sand, animal and vegetable matter, and gravel was cleansed to create the highest quality of clay. It was made pliable after being warmed in the hot sun and then stomped on. It required a great deal of kneading and manipulation to mold it into the desired form for use. Molding took place on a flat surface or by using a potter's wheel. Pottery was dried in the sun until it turned elastic and could be smoothed to the desired texture. Children will create pots and think about the various forms and uses long ago. Because pottery makes a nice gift, this project would fit well with Week 1, which tells about the Christians eating together, and Weeks 2, 3, and 6 when talking about reaching out to others.

Length: This project will take two to three weeks, depending on the complexity of the pottery being made. The amount of clay listed in "Supplies" will make ten 4" pots.

Supplies: Pictures of Bible-time pottery objects, 5 pounds of air-drying clay (available at a craft store), plastic to cover work tables, tempera paints, brushes, water, and cleanup items

Directions: There are a variety of clay items that may be produced by students wanting to participate in this project. Different shaped pots can be formed, oil lamps can be created, or medallions can be made. Encourage students to use their own imaginations when molding items. After the pottery is shaped, set it aside to dry thoroughly, at least a week. After it is dry, you may paint it with tempera paints.

If you decide to expose children to a potter's wheel, be sure to use air-drying clay that you can purchase from a craft store. It would be wise to have someone experienced in making pottery to help you utilize a pottery wheel.

Questions: As students make, mold, and paint their pottery creations, ask these questions: Why was pottery making an important job in Bible times? What are the different materials we use today to substitute for the pottery of the past?

Optional Kindergarten Supplies: Play-Doh

Kindergarten Suggestion: Young people especially enjoy working with their hands. Because clay can be messy and difficult to work with, you may wish to provide younger children with Play-Doh. Play-Doh is a great substitute for clay and can be rolled, molded, and shaped into as many items as clay. Provide Bible storybooks for children to observe while molding their Play-Doh, and then invite them to create some of the items they see in the pictures. Ask them to compare the items they make to the items we use today. Compare the differences and similarities.

7. SPICE BOX PROJECT

Goal: Children will create spice boxes and learn about the various spices, herbs, and fragrances used in worship. Spice boxes were made of silver or fine wood (such as balsa). Inside, different spices were placed for people to sniff. The fragrance then became a remembrance of the joy of the Sabbath and how incense used to be burned in the temple during Bible times. This project would tie in well with Week 7's emphasis on prayer, praise, and corporate worship. Because of its complexity, this project is suggested for older kids.

Length: This project will take any number of weeks, dependent upon the complexity of box carving.

Supplies: Reference books that contain information on Bible-time spices, balsa wood cut in advance, hinges for the lid (two hinges per box, available in hardware stores), screwdrivers (or drill, depending on the hardness of the wood), wood glue (or small tack nails and hammers if you prefer), and wood-carving tools

In Advance: You will need six wood pieces for each box. Cut four pieces that are 6" x 4" and two pieces that are 4" x 4". If you will be using the tack nails and hammers, you may need to alter the size of your wood pieces for nailing the box parts together.

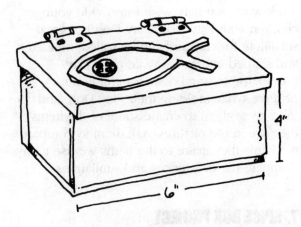

Directions: You will need to have an adult familiar with wood carving and carpentry to guide the children in this project group. Provide Bible-time pictures of worship, and see if students can find spice boxes in them. Research a variety of different spices to find their origin, and which ones were popularly used in Bible times. Students may assemble boxes by following these directions:

1. Provide students with wood-carving tools to carve Bible-time symbols on the box pieces. You will need someone familiar with wood carving available at all times.

2. When carving is done, place the bottom of the box on its side. Glue first one end and then the other to the bottom.

3. When these are dry, turn the box right side up and glue on the front and the back. Set aside to dry completely, at least one week.

4. Attach top of box using hinges, screws, and a screwdriver.

5. Select a fragrant spice such as cinnamon to place inside the box when the project is completed. When students take their boxes home, tell them to think of what they are learning during the Adventure each time they smell the fragrance.

Questions: As spice boxes are made, ask these questions: What are some of the similarities and differences in worship practices during Bible times and today? (Kids will need to research such things as the types of songs sung, how prayers were said, where people met to worship, length of services, and so on.) Why was it important to obtain an agreeable fragrance to place inside the spice box? What did the spice remind people of?

Optional Kindergarten Supplies: Spices, fruits, perfumes, drawing paper, and crayons

Kindergarten suggestion: Kindergartners will enjoy sampling a variety of fragrances. Provide an array of different scents from spices to fruits and perfumes. Ask the children which scents are pleasant, and which ones are not. Encourage them to draw pictures of things that God created that smell good. They can include anything from foods to their favorite flower.

8. BIBLE-TIME METAL PROJECT

Goal: Young people will have an opportunity to work with metal, an important item in Bible times. Mining and metalworking were trades that flourished throughout the Roman Empire. Gold is thought to be the first metal used because of the ease in casting it. Gold, copper, iron, and lead are among the metals mentioned in the Bible. Different metals were used to make tools, vases, jewelry, blocks, pipes, weapons, and disks. Young people will learn not only about different metals and how they were used, but can also make wall hangings or jewelry from metal.

Length: This project will take at least three to four weeks, and perhaps more, depending on the complexity of the projects created.

Supplies: A copy of the Hebrew letters and Bible-time symbols, drawing paper, pencils, aluminum pie pans, a hard surface that will not be damaged by nails, different-sized nails, and string

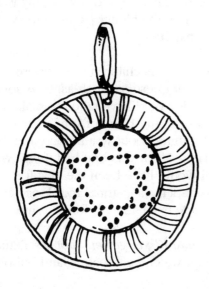

Directions: An adult or older teen should supervise this project. Begin by allowing kids to research Hebrew letters and Bible-time symbols. Distribute drawing paper and have the kids sketch out practice patterns and/or letters to transfer to their pie pans. Tape the preferred pattern and/or letters onto the inside of the pie pan. Have students punch holes, using nails, at short, equal distances in the pie pan to outline their patterns. (Make sure the pie pans are on a hard surface which cannot be damaged by nails. And remind children to watch carefully as they punch holes so as not to poke a finger.) Different hole sizes can be made by using different-sized nail tips. Complete the hanging by punching a small hole in the top of the pie pan to attach string to hang.

Questions: As students research Bible-time symbols and punch out their patterns, ask these questions: How are Bible-time metal products different from the metal products we use today? (Children will need to use reference materials to research this.) What items were made from metal? Why is metal a better material to use than the plastics of today? Why is it not? Also talk with the children about the meanings of their Christian symbols or Hebrew letters.

Optional Kindergarten Supplies: Different-shaped cardboard patterns, yarn, and peg boards and pegs

Kindergarten Suggestion: Working with metal will be too difficult and potentially unsafe for really young children. They may, however, wish to create similar art of the time by designing a pattern out of their favorite shape (heart, square, cross, star). Provide peg boards and pegs for children to insert and copy their patterns onto. For added color, give them yarn to wrap around the pegs.

9. PAPYRUS-MAKING PROJECT

Goal: Kids will learn about writing in Bible times by making their own paper to resemble paper made from papyrus. Other things that were used for writing in Bible times were stone tablets, clay, metal, wooden tablets coated with wax, and parchment. This project works well with the stories in Weeks 4 and 8 about Paul (because he wrote much of the New Testament).

Length: This project will take a minimum of two weeks.

Supplies: Pictures of writing implements, items that writing was done on, and scribes from Bible times; newspapers, water, blotter paper (available at office supply stores), liquid starch, bucket, water source, egg beater or fork, rubber dishpan, a piece of finely meshed screen (small enough to fit inside the dishpan but which can be laid across the dishpan to allow for draining), and a rolling pin

Directions:

1. Tear a page of newspaper into small pieces. Drop them into a bucket and add 2 cups of warm water.

2. Beat this mixture vigorously with an egg beater or fork to make pulp.

3. Mix 2 teaspoons of liquid starch into the pulp mixture.

4. In a rubber dishpan, spread the pulp on top of a finely meshed screen inside the pan.

5. As you lift out the screen, allow the mixture to drain for two minutes.

6. Lay several pieces of newspaper on top of each other, and end with a piece of blotter paper. Set the screen, pulp side up, onto the blotter paper. Put another piece of blotter paper on top of the pulp and then lay several more newspapers on top of that.

7. Take a rolling pin and roll it over the top of the newspapers to squeeze out all the excess water from the pulp.

8. Gently remove the top newspapers. Turn all the remaining papers over together and remove the newspapers, blotter, and screen.

9. Put dry blotter paper on top of the pulp once again. Allow pulp to dry overnight (at least). Peel off the blotter paper to reveal the recycled papyrus.

Questions: As children are working with the pulp ask questions such as: How long do you think it would have taken to make enough paper to write the Book of John? What was one good thing about writing on paper made from plants? What was one bad thing? Which material would have been the best for writing: papyrus paper, clay, stone, metal, or parchment (made from animal skins)? Why?

Optional Kindergarten Supplies: Extra buckets of water, egg beaters, and bubble bath

Kindergarten Suggestion: Young children will enjoy the messy paper-making process as much as the older kids will. While they are waiting for their turn to help, you may want to provide extra buckets of water, bubble bath, and egg beaters for making bubbles in the water.

► ADVENTURE-RELATED PROJECT OPTIONS ◄

The following projects relate well to one or more of the weekly sessions. They are specifically connected to the Bible story or the Scripture memory verse and will act as an excellent reinforcement in getting the lesson across. It is recommended that you use these projects in addition to the Bible-time projects previously mentioned in this section.

1. QUILTING PROJECT

Goal: Children will create a patch quilt representing things they have learned during the Adventure. The quilt can then be donated to the church as a gift, or given to someone in need of a blanket.

Length: Quilt squares will take one week each. However, the quilt will not be finished until Week 8. It is best to start this project during Week 1.

Supplies: Solid-colored fabric squares 6" x 4", fabric crayons (available at craft stores), embroidery threads and needles, scissors, and a sewing machine (optional)

Directions: To do this project, you will need kids willing to spend time at this project site creating individual patches, as well as kids willing to put the patches together to create the final quilt product. Because children will be sewing, you will need to have an adult. You may wish to have this person be an experienced quilter on hand. Quilt squares can be designed in a number of different ways. Younger children may wish to make simple designs using fabric crayons, while older students may wish to try some easy embroidery. Encourage kids to create pictures or symbols that reflect the Adventure Action Steps. Those steps are:

Week 1	Listen to others the way Jesus would
Week 2	Say good things about your church
Week 3	Be caring and make a new friend
Week 4	Put your talents to use
Week 5	Clean up garbage thoughts and actions
Week 6	Take care of the world and its people
Week 7	Meet God in prayer and praise
Week 8	Give thanks that Jesus is alive

In Week 6 or 7 you will want to gather all quilt squares and have kids begin to attach them together either by sewing machine or hand. (Be sure to have an adult supervising.)

Questions: As children work to put together the quilt and design different patches, ask questions like these: Which Action Step are you working on this week? Which Action Step is hard for you? Why? Who could we give our quilt to?

Optional Kindergarten Supplies: Construction paper squares, markers, and tape

Kindergarten Suggestion: Have kids make a paper quilt. They can draw designs on paper squares and attach them together with tape.

2. BIBLE-TIME SCRIBING PROJECT

Goal: Children will have the opportunity to become scribes by working with the Greek alphabet, Roman numerals, and Christian symbols of Bible times. You may wish to use this project to reinforce the Bible Blueprint Memory Verses. If you made papyrus, kids will enjoy writing on it with their quills. This project could work well with Week 2.

Length: This project will take one or two weeks to complete.

Supplies: Copies of the Greek alphabet and Roman numerals, goose or chicken feathers (available at craft stores), sharp scissors, India ink (available at an art or office supply store), felt-tip markers, scrolls (made from attaching paper to dowels), and papyrus (if made as a Bible-time project earlier)

Directions: Provide research materials for students that allow them to see the Greek alphabet, Roman numerals, and Christian symbols of the time. These were all utilized to record history and create scrolls of information.

Scribing was performed at one time with feather quills. Many children will enjoy experimenting with quills, while others will become easily frustrated. Provide felt tip markers for those who do not wish to work with quills. To make quills:

Cut the quill at an angle as shown in the diagram. Then slit the point about 1/4" to 1/2".

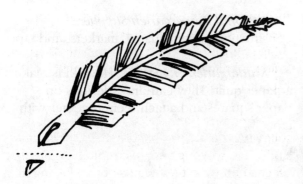

Dip in India ink and use carefully. (Have an adult or older teen on hand to supervise.)

Kids could practice the letters of the Greek alphabet, write the memory verse of the day, or design a scroll that says something good about their church.

Questions: While the students research symbols and lettering, and practice their scribing, ask these questions: What are your favorite Christian symbols? Why? What do they represent? How is working with papyrus and quills different from the way we record information today? How is it similar?

Optional Kindergarten Supplies: Pictures of early Christian symbols, tempera paints, brushes, cleanup items, and paper

Kindergarten Suggestion: It will be too difficult for younger children to learn new numbers and letters because they're just getting a feel for the ones we use today! Focus on Christian symbols, showing various illustrations that you can find. Be sure to explain what each symbol means. Select simple symbols such as a fish or a cross and encourage children to make painted pictures of them.

3. CANDLE-MAKING PROJECT

Goal: Children will create a Havdalah candle to remind them that Jesus is the light of the world (John 8:12), and that he wants them to let their light shine to others. The Jewish people use the Havdalah candle in their celebration of the Sabbath. This project works well in Week 2 when children are encouraged to get the word out to their friends about Jesus. And because candles are still used in worship today, this project would also go well with Week 7 in which children learn about prayer and praise.

Length: This project will take one week to complete.

Supplies (per child): Long, thin candle tapers (2–4 depending on how thick you want your candle), a cooking source, a tea kettle filled with water, 4 oz. air-drying clay (available at craft stores), and toothpicks or other sharp instruments to etch designs in the clay

Directions: You will need to have an adult present to guide the use of the boiling water and to make sure no one gets burned. Take two to four long, thin candle tapers and soften by holding them above steam from a boiling kettle. After tapers have softened enough to braid, do so by starting at the bottom and working slowly upward toward the wick end. Lay braided candles in a safe place and let them harden.

Then hand kids clay to mold holders for their candles. Make sure the opening they leave for the candle is the correct diameter. Kids may then want to etch a design in the clay. Set holders aside to dry. They should dry at least one week.

Questions: As students work to create their candles and holders ask questions like these: What are the different references to light in the Bible? (God made the light/Genesis 1:3–5; Jesus is the light/John 8:12; Let your light shine/Matthew 5:14–16; and so on.) How can you let your light shine to others? Why is it important to praise God in worship and prayer?

Optional Kindergarten Supplies: Chenille wires, Play-Doh, orange tissue paper, and tape

Kindergarten Suggestion: Tell younger students why light is an important word in our Bible. Explain to them that Jesus talks about himself as being a light and that he wants us to be lights, too. Help them understand how they can be lights for Jesus. Provide a variety of craft materials for them to work with to create make-believe candles of their own. Chenille wires may be braided and stuck into Play-Doh bases to shape a candle. Use bright orange tissue paper as a flame.

4. BREAD-BAKING PROJECT

Goal: Children will make bread similar to what people ate in Bible times. During Bible times, bread was generally made from wheat flour or barley meal. Barley was less expensive and used by those who had little money to spare. Baking took place by placing bread on a flat stone over an open fire. Bread was always broken and never cut. Loaves were often shaped like spoons to dip into other foods and sauces. Most loaves were thin, flat disks. The average person consumed three to four loaves each day. This project would fit well with the Bible story for Week 1 or the Action Step for Week 3.

Length: This project will take one session.

Supplies: Mixing bowls, mixing spoons and measuring spoons, measuring cups, an egg beater, 8" or 9" pie plate, a rolling pin, something to grease the pie plate with, waxed paper, butter, a knife, recipe items, a grain mill (optional), paper, and markers

Directions: Have children make bread by following this recipe. Be sure to exercise caution when working with ovens, and require that all children wash their hands before joining in this project. If you have the resources, provide a grain mill and let students experiment with grinding natural flour.

Bread recipe:
- 1-1/2 cups barley flour
- 1-1/2 teaspoons baking powder
- 1 tablespoon brown sugar
- 2 tablespoons softened butter
- 1 tablespoon granulated sugar
- 1/2 teaspoon salt
- 1/2 cup milk
- 1 egg

Sift together dry ingredients. Beat egg and milk with an egg beater. Add softened butter and beat well. Mix together with the dry ingredients. On a floured wax paper surface, roll dough into a smooth circle approximately 1/2" thick. Grease the pie plate and lay the dough inside. Bake at 425 degrees for 15–17 minutes until bread is lightly browned. Cool and serve.

As the bread bakes, explain to students that bread was often a gift to friends. Talk about who in your congregation may enjoy receiving a gift of bread. If you bake extra loaves to give away, have kids write a note to accompany the gift.

Questions: As students make, bake, and eat bread together, ask these questions: How is baking bread today different from the manner in which bread was made during Bible times? Why do we cut bread instead of breaking it today? What are other gifts you could make or give to someone you would like to have as a new friend?

Optional Kindergarten Supplies: Ready-made refrigerator biscuits or rolls, baking sheet, and cinnamon

Kindergarten Suggestion: Bake some ready-to-make refrigerator biscuits or rolls by flattening them with the palm of your hand and sprinkling with cinnamon. Bake at 400 degrees for approximately 10 minutes or until brown. Cool and serve.

5. MOSAIC PROJECT

Goal: Children will become familiar with a popular Bible-time decoration and art. They will make mosaics to depict the Bible story or a symbol to reflect the Bible memory verse. This project will work well with all weeks.

Length: This project will take one week, and will change from week to week.

Supplies: Books showing Bible-time mosaics, construction paper or old wrapping paper, cotton-tipped swabs, glue, drawing paper, and pencils

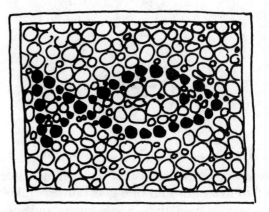

Directions: Obtain some Bible-time art books so that children can have an opportunity to observe mosaics of the past. Provide children with drawing paper and pencils for making sketches of their designs. When they have settled on a design, hand them a piece of construction paper to use as a background. After they have drawn their design, encourage them to cut or tear construction or wrapping paper into small pieces. Instruct them to spread a thin layer of glue over a small area of their design and then, using a cotton-tipped swab dipped in glue, to lift mosaic pieces into place one by one. When done, mosaics will probably need to dry overnight.

Questions: As students put together their mosaics, ask these questions: What does the mosaic say about the Bible story or memory verse for the day? Where is mosaic art still found and seen today? How do mosaics differ from the interior and exterior decorations within your home and community today?

Kindergarten Suggestion: Allow younger children to do a mosaic project too, but with larger mosaic pieces. You may also need to suggest designs they might make to help them review what they've been learning in the Adventure.

6. TIE-DYE CLOTH PROJECT

Goal: Children will have an experience with dyeing fabric to interest them or remind them of the story of Lydia. This project will work well in Week 6 or 7.

Length: This project will take approximately two weeks to finish.

Supplies: Newspaper, pre-washed white cotton squares or T-shirts, large pot (not aluminum), large spoon, fabric dye, rubber bands, hot water source, wooden spoon or tongs, latex gloves, clothespins, and some type of clothesline

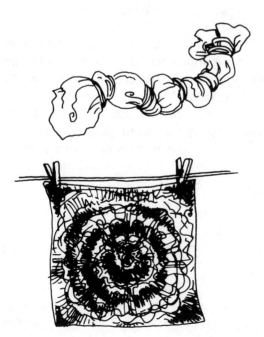

Directions: Because you will be using boiling water, an adult or older teen needs to be supervising this activity. Using rubber bands, section off parts of the squares. Then follow the directions for dyeing cotton cloth on your packaged dye. After dyeing, rinse the squares in cold water. (Be sure to use a wooden spoon or tongs to lift the squares out of the hot dye water into cold water.) Take off rubber bands and rinse again. Squeeze out water and hang to dry.

Questions: While kids are working with their tie-dyes ask questions such as: How do you think they dyed cloth in Bible-times? Where do you think they got the purple dye for the cloth Lydia sold? What other things could you tie-dye?

7. MEZUZAH PROJECT

Goal: Children will construct Mezuzahs that will contain a scroll inscribed with Deuteronomy 6:4–5. This project will help kids to remember the importance of meeting with the Master Builder, the Training Topic for Week 7.

Length: This project will take one to two weeks.

Supplies: A pre-painted or solid-colored shoe box for each child, tempera paint, brushes, cleanup items, 1/2" dowels cut into 6"–8" lengths, glue, paper to fit dowels, markers, Jewish reference and/or holiday craft books

In Advance: Pre-paint shoe boxes using spray paint.

Directions: A Mezuzah is a small box that appeared on the doorpost of Jewish homes. Family members and visitors alike would touch it each time they entered or left the home to remind them of God's great law contained within. The law, known as the Shema from Deuteronomy 6:4–5, was found inscribed on a scroll. Show kids pictures of a Mezuzah, the Shema, and Hebrew lettering. Then encourage them to paint their boxes with Jewish symbols and Hebrew letters.

While the boxes are drying, children will create Shemas to place inside their Mezuzahs. They will need to write Deuteronomy 6:4–5 on paper, then glue the paper to two dowels. When glue is dry, children may roll up their Shema scrolls and place them inside their Mezuzahs. (It may be a good idea to allow scrolls and Mezuzahs one week to dry.)

Questions: As students work to complete their Mezuzahs and Shemas, ask these questions: Why do you think the people felt it was important to place the Mezuzah on their doorpost? Why did they touch it each time they entered or left the house? What are some Christian traditions or customs we practice today? Why? How do you meet with the Master Builder?

Kindergarten Suggestion: Young people will enjoy decorating a cardboard box and putting something inside it. Explain that the Mezuzah was like a memory box that helped people to think about God each time they came home or went somewhere. Have the children make a picture of something God has made that they are thankful for. Tell students to roll it up and put it inside their box. Point out that each time they see their box, they will be reminded of the special things God has given them!

8. CONSTRUCTION CREW BANNER PROJECT

Goal: Children will create banners to represent each week's On–the–Job Training Topic listed on page 49. This project will help reinforce the weekly messages that kids will take home with them.

Length: This project will take one week, but will change each week to reflect the different weekly themes.

Supplies: Butcher or freezer paper, markers, glitter, magazines, scissors, and glue

Directions: Write in big block outline or balloon-shaped letters each Training Topic for the kids to color. You might also draw a symbol to represent each one. Or discuss the symbols with the kids first to get their ideas, and help them draw the symbols (depending on the age and the ability of the kids). Let the children use markers to color the banners, or glue and glitter to decorate them. They may also want to cut out magazine pictures that go with each weekly topic. They can then glue their pictures to the banners to make them colorful. Display each banner in an area where everyone can look forward to seeing it each week.

Questions: Ask the group questions such as these about the topic for the day: What does this week's Training Topic mean? Why is it important? What are some symbols, words, or pictures that come to mind when you think about this message? What picture would help you to remember this Training Topic?

The Adventure Training Topics are:

WEEK	TOPICS	SUGGESTED SYMBOLS
1	Care for each other in God's family	A group of children holding hands or a child holding flowers
2	Get the word out to your friends	A newspaper, TV, or a child with a megaphone
3	Open the door	A child standing by an open door
4	Use your tools well	A musical instrument, sports object, or artist supplies
5	Take out the trash	A Dumpster, child emptying trash can, or trash truck
6	Help in other places	A picture of the world or people from different countries
7	Meet with the Master Builder	A songbook or silhouette of child praying
8	Celebrate the best club ever	A clubhouse or a group of kids jumping up and down

9. WALL FRESCO PAINTING PROJECT

Goal: Children will paint backdrops for upcoming Bible story presentations.

Length: This project can be completed in one week but will change from week to week to reflect the weekly Bible story.

Supplies: Butcher or freezer paper, newspapers, tempera paints, brushes, cleanup items, books showing Bible-time art and scenery, and Bibles

Directions: Show pictures of wall fresco paintings. Encourage children to read upcoming Bible stories and to design appropriate backdrops. (Week 1 is not included as it would be hard for kids to get this backdrop finished in time for the first Bible Story Presentation. The stories that would work best are:

STORIES	SUGGESTED BACKDROPS
Week 3: Acts 10:1–35 (The story of Peter's vision and his visit to Cornelius's house.)	A. Bible-time rooftops B. Inside of a Roman Bible-time home
Week 6: Acts 16:6–15 (The story of the man from Macedonia and Paul's meeting with Lydia.)	A. Room inside a Bible-time home with mat on floor for bed, and wooden furniture B. Outside scene by a river
Week 8: Acts 9:1–19 (The story of Saul's conversion.)	A. Road scene with Damascus in the distance B. Inside of a Jewish Bible-time home

Questions: While kids work on their paintings, ask these questions: What did Bible-times landscapes look like? How are they different than our landscapes today? What did Bible-time homes look like? Where did Bible-time artists get their paints and other supplies? What scenes would be best for each story?

▶ OVERVIEW ◀

On-the-Job Training Topic: Care for each other in God's family
Action Step: Listen to others the way Jesus would
Bible Story: Acts 2:42–47; Acts 4:32–35
Memory Verse: 1 John 4:11 (NIV)

GETTING STARTED

See "Ready to Begin—Administrative Information" on pages 11–14 for an overview of the children's Adventure program and for suggestions concerning attendance and the selection, identification, and naming of the children's small groups.

As the children arrive, they should stop by the Adventure check-in table to record their attendance, pick up their color-coded name tags, and meet their small group leaders. Because of the construction theme you might want to furnish each child with a paper hardhat (available at card and party stores). The first day of the Adventure can be confusing for some children, so delegate time for orienting children to the program.

If you have chosen to offer Bible-Time Projects first, explain what is available and where, before you send kids on their way. If you have selected Bible Story Time as your opening activity, be sure to offer an introductory activity like singing as children gather for the presentation.

Bible-Time Projects

Refer to "Bible-Time Projects" (p. 27) and "How Long Do I Spend on Each Part of the Session?" (p.9). Plan to have one project worktable and one adult leader for every 10–12 children. During Week 1, children will need an opportunity to preview each project before making their initial decision of where to work. Because of the need for introduction, children will not have a chance to accomplish much during the first week. But don't worry; this will give the kids something to look forward to in the following sessions.

Bible Story Time

Have the children gather in a large group and sit with their small group leaders. For ideas on how to make Bible Story Time more effective, see pages 16–17.

WEEKLY ACTIVITIES

Welcome the children to the 50-Day Adventure. Introduce yourself, and recognize any first-time visitors. Use this time for making announcements, acknowledging birthdays, or taking an offering. If you are using this curriculum for your children's church program, you may prefer to take the offering during worship time.

SETTING THE SCENE

Things You'll Need: Safety cones, construction worker clothes (an orange safety vest, work boots, hardhat [may be purchased at a party store], and jeans), hammer, nails, paint and brushes, a sawhorse, nine pieces of flat wood, and one 2" x 4" for attaching flat wood pieces, a construction work boot, and a copy of the Action Step (see "Preparation" section)

Preparation

To set the stage, make or borrow several safety cones and a sawhorse with "Construction Zone" lettered across it. Dress in construction crew work gear (a bright orange safety vest, jeans, work boots, hardhat or something similar). Each week you will challenge the group with an Action Step related to an On-the-Job Training Topic. Paint each week's On-the-Job Training Topic large enough for kids to read it on a separate piece of wood. Each week you will add one of these wood pieces by nailing it to a wooden post. Select a location to place this post each week. Then, write each week's Action Step on a piece of paper and roll it up. Tuck it inside the boot and set the boot next to the Training Notice Post. This will make your construction zone come alive with the Adventure theme "Building a place where you belong!" Each week, you will also use a construction tool to introduce the Bible Blueprint Memory Verse.

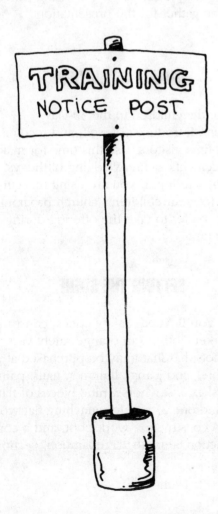

Topic Introduction

Good morning! Is everybody ready to become a member of the G. H. Construction Crew? I hope so! But first, can anyone tell me what the G. H. stands for? Allow kids time to respond. **God's House! God wants his house (the church) to be a place where everyone can feel loved and accepted. But that doesn't always happen. Why?** Allow kids time to respond. Some things they might suggest are cliques, unkindness, being left out, being made fun of, or not knowing how to make friends. **That's right. Sometimes when kids come to church they feel more unloved or unaccepted than in school. Well, whether you have been one of those kids who have felt left out at church, or one who was upset when you saw other kids treated badly at church, this Adventure is for you. During the 50-Day Adventure, you and thousands of other people will tackle the job of making God's house (the church) a better place for everyone. As a part of the crew, you'll learn eight On-the-Job Training Topics and be asked to practice eight important Action Steps. These steps are things you can use not only at church, but at home and school as well. These steps will help you to love God and others better. Any ideas what those Action Steps might be?** Allow time for kids to respond. **Good ideas!** Look at watch. **But we need to get busy. There's so much to do! The first thing I need to do is to ask someone to help me put up our first On-the-Job Training Topic.** Pull out hammer, nails, and the On-the-Job Training Topic sign for this week. Invite a child to come and hold the sign while you nail it onto the Training Notice Post. **Now, can anyone read it for the group?** Choose a child to read the topic and then have the group read it again. **"Care for each other in God's family." Hmm! How do we do that?** Allow time for children to respond. **Let's see how our Action Step says we can care for others.** Invite a child to pull the Action Step out of the boot. Read it to the group. **"Listen to others the way Jesus would." That's an interesting one. I think I need some help with that one. And I'm sure that our Bible story will help. Let's watch and listen.**

BIBLE STORY PRESENTATION

Bible Basis:	*Acts 2:42–47;*
	Acts 4:32–35
Characters:	*Ned (or Nancy)*
	Know-It-All
	Believers 1, 2, and 3
Things You'll Need:	*Microphone*
	Bible
	Basket of bread
	Basket of fruit
	Warm coat
	Bible-time costumes
	for Believers
	Cloak/cape for
	Believer 1

Ned: [*To audience*] This is the Nightly News with Ned Know-It-All, live in Jerusalem. [*Believer 1 walks by carrying a basket of bread.*] Excuse me, Ma'am.

Believer 1: [*Stops startled at the interruption.*] I'm sorry, but I must be on my way.

Ned: I'll just keep you a moment. I'm Ned Know-It-All from the Jerusalem News Team. I happen to know that you're a believer in Jesus. Can you tell me where you're going?

Believer 1: I'm going to sell my cloak and give the bread I've baked to people who have none. There are a lot of people who need help, you know. So I really do have to get going. [*Moves to leave.*]

Ned: [*Stops her from leaving by standing in front of her.*] You say you're going to sell your cloak and give bread to the needy. Why would anyone do that?

Believer 1: Surely YOU know, Mr.Know-It-All [*Ned gives questioning look.*] The apostles (Jesus' followers) have been teaching us how to care for others the way Jesus would.

Ned: [*Confused*] How do you do that?

Believer 1: By being observant. Watching everywhere we go for people who might need help. Listening carefully when our friends talk about things that are bothering them, then asking if we can help. Listening at church to hear if anyone is sick or in need of special prayer.

Ned: But what does that have to do with selling your cloak?

Believer 1: You really don't know it all, do you?

Ned: I guess not.

Believer 1: Well, that's OK. Now, back to what I'm doing. You see, I heard at church that there were some people who didn't have enough to eat. SO, I prayed and asked God to help me figure out what I could do to help. That's when I realized that I had two cloaks, one more than I really needed. With the money I could make from selling one of the cloaks I could buy extra wheat to bake bread for those who were hungry. [*Looks up as if looking to see the sun.*] Oh, my, I could go on and on, but I need to be going. Have to get home before dark, you know. Perhaps you'd like to stop by my house later and break bread with my family and me.

Ned: Break bread?

Believer 1: We'd like to share a meal with you.

Ned: Sounds great! I'd love to come.

Believer 1: I'll see you this evening, then. But right now I have to run. [*Exits*]

Ned: Now THAT'S a nice neighbor. [*Believers 2 and 3 walk by carrying a Bible, a basket of fruit, and a warm coat.*] Excuse me, just a moment please! [*They stop.*] I'm Ned Know-It-All with the Nightly News, and I need to ask you a few questions. You're both believers in Jesus, right?

Believer 2: Yes, how can we be of help to you?

Ned: Can you tell me where you're going with all these things?

Believer 3: Are you in need of them?

Ned: Well, no . . .

Believer 3: That's right, it wasn't Ned Need-It-

All, it was Ned Know-It-All.

Believer 2: We're on our way to tell others the good news of Jesus' love!

Believer 3: And to share what we have with people who need our help.

Ned: But if you share what you have, you won't have enough left for yourselves.

Believer 2: Not really. You see, if everyone cared for one another all the time, then no one would ever be in need.

Ned: [*Thinking about this.*] Naturally.

Believer 2: Ned, are you in need of anything?

Ned: Well, I could use a couple of nice friends to tell me about this Jesus.

Believer 3: Why don't you come with us?

Ned: Now?

Believer 2: Never a better time than the present.

Ned: All I needed was a nudge. [*Back to the audience.*] This is Not-Necessarily-Know-It-All Ned with the Nightly News admitting that I'm just new at this myself. [*Believers 2 and 3 have started to leave.*] Hey! Wait for me! Now tell me more about this Jesus . . . [*They exit.*]

COMPREHENSION QUESTIONS

Briefly discuss these questions with the children to clarify the main ideas in the Bible story presentation.

• **What had the apostles taught the believers?** (About caring for others the way Jesus would.)

• **Believer 1 told some ways we could do this. What were those ways?** (By being observant. Watching everywhere we go for people who might need help. Listening carefully when our friends talk about things that are bothering them, then asking if we can help. Listening at church to hear if anyone is sick or in need of special prayer.)

• **What caring things did the believers do for Ned?** (Invited him to share a meal, asked him if he needed anything, and asked if he wanted to hear about Jesus.)

BIBLE BLUEPRINT MEMORY VERSE

Things You'll Need: Blueprint (you could get one from an architect or contractor), wooden box with a removable lid (this week the lid is screwed on), a screwdriver, a Bible, and a copy of the verse

"Dear friends, since God so loved us, we also ought to love one another."
1 John 4:11 (NIV)

Each week the children will have an opportunity to learn a new Bible Blueprint Memory Verse. Using a tool to get into the Bible Blueprint Verse box will be a fun way to reinforce the construction theme. To make the wooden box, follow the directions for making the spice box in the Bible-time projects section, pages 39–40. Be sure to adjust finished box size to fit the Bible you will be putting inside each week.

You will need a blueprint for this week only. You will also need the wooden box large enough to hold a Bible. The box will need a lid that can be opened in a variety of different ways (using different construction tools). Each week you will use a different tool. Write the Bible memory verse on a piece of paper large enough for everyone to read it. Fold it, put it in the Bible, and place it inside the box. This week, you will need to SCREW the lid on and will need a screwdriver to get inside.

Does anyone know what a blueprint is? Allow children to respond. **That's right. Construction workers use them for directions when they are building. God has provided us with blueprints to help us make the church a better place, too. These blueprints are in the Bible.**

Today, I brought a special box with me. What do you think is inside? Allow children to guess. **Inside this box is a Bible Blueprint Memory Verse. Who can tell me why it's a good idea to memorize Bible verses?** Allow time for children to respond. Answers might include: it helps to remember verses when you're having a hard time, you can't always carry your Bible around with you, and so on. **That's right. Now, let's dig into our box and see this week's verse. Can anybody guess which tool I need to get the lid off?** Display the box for children to see. Allow time to respond. **It's a good thing I have my screwdriver.** Begin to loosen the lid screws. Ask for assistance from a child.

Screwdrivers are terrific tools for fixing, repairing, and tightening, or for opening things up! There! Open the box and take the Bible out. Pull the paper with the verse on it out of the Bible for everyone to see. **"Dear friends, since God so loved us, we also ought to love one another." 1 John 4:11. It's easy to love some people and harder to love others. But God wants us to love everyone in God's family. Who is in God's family?** (Other believers.) **What are some ways we can love them?** Invite the children to name specific ways we can show our love. Answers might include being friendly with kids that go to other churches or church clubs, inviting new kids at church to be a part of our group, doing nice things for the older people in our church, and so on. **Let's repeat the verse aloud. Now let's try to sing it.** Teach them to sing the verse to the tune of "Row, Row, Row Your Boat":

> Dear friends, de-ar friends
> Since God so loved us,
> We al-so ought to love
> One a-no-o-ther.

The younger children can learn a shortened version of the verse: "Love one another." If you choose to have them sing it to the same tune as the older kids, it could go like this:

> Love, love, lo-ve, love
> One a-no-o-ther,
> Love, love, love, love
> One a-no-o-ther.

If you choose to have the younger children learn a shorter version of the verse, you may wish to split the group in half during the Bible Blueprint presentation. Another option is to have the small group leaders work on the verse when they meet with the children (if the groups are age-graded).

Life Application
Small Group Time

For instructions on working with the small groups, see "Tips for Small Group Leaders" on page 23, and the Life Application section under "Ready to Begin—Weekly Leader Information" on page 18. Small group leaders will need a copy of the Life Application Page (59–60) to lead their groups this week. They will need this page at least one week ahead of time.

Each small group leader will need to make a poster of the Adventure Prayer on page 24 and individual posters of the Action Steps and On-the-Job Training Topics. Making the posters in the shapes of tools will help to add to the construction theme. You will find a complete list of supplies needed on the Life Application Page for each week. You will also need to do some preplanning if you choose to have your small groups involved in a missions project during Week 6. Think about having your children bring in a special offering, toys, or clothes for a homeless shelter or for children overseas. You may be able to get ideas for projects from missionaries your church supports.

Children's Church Worship

Things You'll Need: *Bible Memory Toolbox* cassette, cassette player, and an offering container

If you are using this section, be sure to allow kids a short time to stand up and stretch in between activities. You might also want to include some active songs during the singing time.

SINGING

Choose music that correlates with this week's On-the-Job Training Topic (Care for each other in God's family) and the Action Step (Listen to others the way Jesus would). To reinforce this week's Bible Blueprint Verse, teach "We Ought to Love One Another," page 119 of this book. (Also found on the *Bible Memory Toolbox* sing-along cassette tape. See page 128 for ordering.)

CRITTER COUNTY STORY

Through the familiar and friendly Critter County characters, the children can see this week's theme in action and be motivated to listen to and care for others. This week's story begins on page 57.

OFFERING

One way children can learn to worship and respond to God is by giving. If you are using this curriculum for a children's church program, you may prefer to take the offering now instead of during the Weekly Activities portion of the Bible Story Time. Encourage children to thank God for something either verbally or silently as the offering plate passes by.

PRAISE AND PRAYER

Talking to God is the best way to communicate what we feel, need, are thankful for, and want help with. Because children may feel nervous about praying out loud, they will need help and guidance in how to do this comfortably. Remind everyone that there are no "right" or "wrong" things to say to God. He listens to everything we say, and always knows just what we mean when we say it.

Each week when you pray together, you will gradually be shifting more of the prayer responsibility from you to the children. To help kids get started, offer a sentence, and then ask them to repeat it. Use a prayer such as: "Thank you, God, for loving us." (Repeat) "Thank you, God, for taking care of us." (Repeat) "Show me how to love my friends at church." (Repeat) "Help me listen when they tell me about their problems." (Repeat) "Help me know how to help them. Amen." (Repeat)

Midweek Extras

Things You'll Need: Copies of game cards (as described) for each child, pencils, beans, a cassette player, and the *Bible Memory Toolbox* cassette

If you are using this curriculum for a midweek children's program or as a combined Sunday School/Children's Church program during the 50-Day Adventure, you may wish to add these fun activities to your time together.

GAME

Love One Another Match-up

Provide each group with a pencil and a piece of paper that has 25 squares on it. Draw a heart in the center square. Tell children to scramble about, asking everyone in the group to sign their name on one of the squares. If you have fewer than 25 children to work with, go around two or three times until all the squares have been filled.

Next, have each child write his or her name on a small piece of paper and put it into a brown paper bag. Then, one at a time, draw out names from the bag. Children should place a bean on the name of the person called each time that name appears on the child's grid. When a child gets five in a row in any direction, he or she should shout, "Love One Another!"

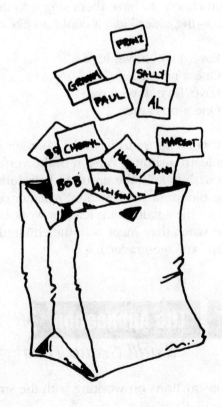

Adjustment for Younger Ages

Suggest that the older children and younger children work together as a team. (It's a great way to show love for one another.) Older children can be responsible for writing and reading, younger children can be in charge of placing the beans. The team should shout "Love One Another" together when they have five beans in a row.

SINGING

Singing is a fun way to praise God. Make use of the songs included in this book, beginning on page 119. The songs in this book are also found on the *Bible Memory Toolbox* sing-along cassette tape. Be sure to learn the song "We Ought to Love One Another" based on this week's Bible Blueprint Verse. And remember to include some active songs to give kids an opportunity to move around.

CRITTER COUNTY STORY

The friendly animals of Critter County bring this week's Action Step and On-the-Job Training Topic to life.

The Best Gift

There was a quiet hush in the halls of the Critter County Hospital. The nurses and doctors were busy doing everything they could to help the little bunny. The Love Birds were waiting and praying in the visitors' lounge. Seated next to them were Mr. and Mrs. Skunk. Mrs. Skunk was wearing her favorite perfume. Sydney the squirrel sat quietly in the corner with the bunny's parents.

A little after 9:00 in the evening, Grandmother Mouse came into the waiting room. She was dressed in her fresh nurse's uniform, white hose, and shoes. She spoke ever so softly. "The doctor has asked me to come and talk with all of you. It seems Bouncy the bunny is not doing so well. We need to find someone in Critter County who can keep Bouncy company tomorrow morning. The doctors think the company will help Bouncy feel better."

"Hey, what about her sister? Where is Beautiful? I would think that she'd be glad to help," suggested Sydney.

"Good idea!" answered Bouncy's mom. "Her dad can ask her when he gets home." And with that, the daddy bunny headed toward home. As soon as the daddy bunny got home, he went straight to Beautiful's room and found her lying on her canopy bed with the pink spread. She was sound asleep holding her favorite baby doll. "Beautiful, wake up," he said softly. Beautiful woke up and looked sleepily at her dad. "What's wrong, Dad? Is Bouncy OK?"

"Honey, your sister isn't doing so well. The doctor wants someone to keep her company tomorrow. And your mother and I thought you'd be just the person to cheer Bouncy up."

"Oh, Dad, I'd love to go and help Bouncy. But tomorrow is the class picnic. I just can't miss that."

"I know that would be hard to miss. And there might be someone else who could help. But would you think about it and give me an answer in the morning?" he asked.

"OK," she answered, "See you in the morning."

Daddy gave her a hug and went down to get a snack.

Beautiful couldn't get to sleep. She had a decision to make. She knew that being with Bouncy was a good thing to do, but she wasn't sure she was the right person for the job. And she sure did want to go to that picnic. *Maybe it will rain tomorrow morning*, she thought to herself. *That would help me make my decision.* She thought about Bouncy a lot, wondering what it would be like to be in a hospital. And eventually she went to sleep.

It was a lovely sunny morning when Beautiful woke up. She headed down to the breakfast table. Her dad was having some carrot juice. "Made a decision yet?" Dad asked.

"Yes," answered Beautiful. "I have decided to go to the picnic AND to help Bouncy."

"How are you going to do that?" he asked.

"Well, I'm going to take a picnic to share with Bouncy in the hospital."

"That's a great idea, Beautiful. It's the best gift you could give your sister—yourself and your time! Thanks, honey!"

"You're welcome, Dad. I hope it helps."

And it did!

Life Application Page

For Small Group Leaders

▶ **WEEK ONE** ◀

ON-THE-JOB TRAINING TOPIC:
Care for each other in God's family

ACTION STEP:
Listen to others the way Jesus would

BIBLE STORY:
*Acts 2:42–47;
Acts 4:32–35*

MEMORY VERSE:
1 John 4:11 (NIV)

THINGS YOU'LL NEED:

- Copy of "Tips for Small Group Leaders" from pages 23–24
- Action Step/Training Topic poster (made in advance)
- Children's Journal
- Adventure Prayer poster (made in advance)
- Children's Activity Book
- Newsprint
- Marker
- Chalkboard and chalk

IN ADVANCE:

Make a tool-shaped poster of the Adventure Prayer on page 24. Also make tool-shaped posters of the Action Step and On-the-Job Training Topic.

KID TALK

The purpose of small group time is to pave the way for children to think and talk about today's Bible story. They will share ways to take the message home and talk about how it will affect their lives. Have this week's On-the-Job Training Topic and Action Step displayed. Encourage the KIDS to do the talking. Ask questions like those listed below. Be prepared to share your own examples to get the discussion moving.

• **In our Bible story presentation, how did the believers care for each other?**

• **There are so many church friends who need our care that it is hard to know what to do first. God understands that we can't help everybody. But there are some things we can do. Name some of these things.** (Give a smile or a hug, help with a chore, give clothes and toys to a friend, visit someone who is sick, and so on.)

• **Name some things that God does to show his love for you.**

• **What is something you have done to show love recently? How did it make the person receiving your love feel?**

• **Can you think of someone right now in your church or church club who could use love? What is one way you can show love to that person?** (Write kids' suggestions on the chalkboard or newsprint.)

Talk about this week's On-the-Job Training Topic and Action Step using the posters you made. Explain that God needs everyone in his family to be a part of his crew. Show children the Action Step poster. **Each week you'll be given an opportunity to learn a new Action Step that will help you build God's house into a place where everyone can feel welcomed and loved. Today's Action Step is "Listen to others the way Jesus would." Listening is one way we can show God's love to our friends at church.**

Show sample copies of the Adventure journals and ask which kids have journals at home. (See the "Small Group Tip" following "Prayer Talk.") Explain that as they follow their journals this week, they'll have more fun learning how to use the Action Step they discovered today. Provide information to kids without journals about how to get one. Explain that each week you'll give them a chance to tell each other something about what they're doing in their journals.

PRAYER TALK

Talking to Jesus is an important way to let him know we are listening, learning, and trying to care for one another. Each week we'll pray a prayer that will help us talk to God. If you have an Adventure journal at home, you'll find this prayer in it. Praying this prayer is a good way to show God that you've decided to act on this week's Action Step. It reminds us to be caring members of God's family, and it encourages us to take action.

Call attention to your Adventure Prayer poster at this time. (If time allows, you might let your group make the poster rather than making it yourself ahead of time.) Read the prayer to the children, or read it together, depending on your age-group. Encourage the kids to use this prayer throughout the week as a starting point for talking to God during the 50-Day Adventure.

Before you conclude the prayer time, encourage children to talk to Jesus in their own words. Have them pray for the needs that were mentioned earlier. They may also wish to extend a word of thanks, ask for help or forgiveness, celebrate something good or special, or pray for someone in need.

If time permits, encourage everyone to share something about themselves with the group. (Kids could share their favorite food, pet, school subject, and so on.) This is an excellent way for the group to begin forming relationships and start caring for one another. As the group becomes more comfortable, children will be encouraged to pray for each other.

Small Group Tip

The kids in your church have the option of taking part in the 50-Day Spiritual Adventure on a daily basis by using a journal. The journal for grades 3–6 is called *G. H. Construction Crew*. The activity book for grades K–2 is called *Critter County Clubhouse*. The kids do not need to bring these books to church, but they will get a lot more out of the Adventure if they do the daily journal activities at home. The topics and memory verses are the same as those the kids learn together in the weekly sessions.

During small group time each week, you will be asked to talk with the kids about what they're learning in their journals. This will help everyone keep track of how well they are applying the Action Steps to their lives. Since some of the children may not have their own journals yet, find out from your church's Adventure coordinator how they can get copies.

WEEK two

On-the-Job Training Topic: Get the word out to your friends

Action Step: Say good things about your church

Bible Story: Acts 5:12–16

Memory Verse: Psalm 9:1 (NIV)

GETTING STARTED

As the children arrive, they should stop by the Adventure check-in table to record their attendance, pick up their color-coded name tags, and meet their small group leaders. They can then proceed to work on the Bible-time project of their choice or move to the Bible Story Time with their small group leaders.

 ## Bible-Time Projects

Continue to work on the projects introduced last week. Offer any new projects that correlate with this week's lesson.

 ## Bible Story Time

Gather the children together in a large group with their small group leaders.

WEEKLY ACTIVITIES

Welcome the children back to the Adventure. Proceed by making any necessary announcements, recognizing birthdays, or taking an offering.

SETTING THE SCENE

Things You'll Need: Safety cones, construction worker clothes (an orange safety vest, work boots, hardhat [may be purchased at a party store], and jeans), hammer, nails, paint and brushes, a sawhorse, a piece of flat wood

and the wooden Training Notice Post you started last week, a construction boot, a copy of the Action Step, and a bullhorn (or something similar made from construction paper)

Preparation

Make the area look like a construction site. Dress in your construction crew work gear. Paint this week's On-the-Job Training Topic on a piece of wood. Make it large enough for kids to read, and tuck a copy of this week's Action Step in the boot. Place the boot by the Training Notice Post. Place the bullhorn out of sight but within reach.

Topic Introduction

Good morning! It's great to see all you G. H. Construction Crew workers back again this week. Are you ready to build a place where all God's children can belong? Encourage an energetic response. **So am I! It's really great to be a part of God's crew, isn't it? I think there must be other kids who would like to be on our crew, too.** Nail up topic. **Our On-the-Job Training Topic for this week is "Get the word out to your friends." But how do we get the word out to our neighbors and**

friends at school that church (or church club) is a great place? One thing I thought of was . . . pull out bullhorn and talking into it say, . . . **using one of these! Who knows what this is?** Allow kids to answer as you turn off bull horn. **It's a bullhorn. Sometimes construction bosses use these to talk to crew workers who are up high on a building.** Use bull horn again and say, **But I don't think this is the best way to get the word out that church is a great place. Do you have any better ideas on how we could do that?** Turn off bull horn and allow children to offer ideas. These might include telling friends about the neat things that are happening at church, doing nice things that might open a door for you to talk to people about Jesus, and so on. **You have some great ideas!**

Now, let's see what our Action Step says to do. Invite a child to pull the Action Step out of the boot. **It says, "Say good things about your church." That's one way to get the word out and cause people to want to check out the church. What are some things you could say or do that would make other people want to come and learn about God here?** Allow for children to respond. **Last week's Action Step was about listening to others the way Jesus would. This week we want to be showing and telling others the good things happening at church (or church club) so that they will want to come, too. Now let's learn how people in Bible days got the word out.**

BIBLE STORY PRESENTATION

Bible Basis: Acts 5:12–16
Things You'll Need: *Copy of choral reading*

Today's story presentation is a Choral Reading presented by a leader and responded to by the children. The leader should begin by dividing the audience into two parts, Group I and Group II. Rehearse the following parts with them:

Group I will say: **What is a child of God to do?** *(Hold hands out to the side and shrug shoulders.)*
Group II will say: **Get the good word out to you and you!** *(Point up, then to two people.) Rehearse these lines with each group so they will respond with their line when pointed to.*

After Jesus' death and resurrection, the apostles (Jesus' followers) continued spreading the good news about him. They were able to perform miraculous signs. Crowds would often gather in the streets, bringing with them sick people so that they might be healed. As the apostles spread the good news of Jesus, more and more people came to believe in him. And many who believed began to meet in groups that were eventually called churches. It was in these churches that new believers learned about Jesus and his love from the other believers. The apostles "got the word out" by doing good things for others. Now, let's think about some of the good things we could do for or say to others as we review the story together.

Leader: People came from every town. [*Point to Group I, then II.*]
Group I: What is a child of God to do?
Group II: Get the good word out to you and you!
Leader: The crowds would gather all around.
Group I: What is a child of God to do?
Group II: Get the good word out to you and you!
Leader: The apostles talked of Jesus' love.
Group I: What is a child of God to do?
Group II: Get the good word out to you and you!

Leader: God sent miracles from above.

Group I: What is a child of God to do?

Group II: Get the good word out to you and you!

Leader: Sick people were healed through and through.

Group I: What is a child of God to do?

Group II: Get the good word out to you and you!

Leader: Many people believed, and the numbers grew.

Group I: What is a child of God to do?

Group II: Get the good word out to you and you!

Leader: Now, there's something God calls us to do!

Group I: What is a child of God to do?

Group II: Get the good word out to you and you!

Leader: 'Cause we're all a part of God's work crew.

Group I: What is a child of God to do?

Group II: Get the good word out to you and you!

Leader: What?

Group II: Get the good word out to you and you!

Leader: Everybody—

Groups I and II: Get the good word out to you and you!

COMPREHENSION QUESTIONS

Briefly discuss these questions with the children to clarify the main ideas in the Bible story presentation.

• **What did the apostles do that got others interested in the church?** (They met together, talked about Jesus, did miracles, and healed many.)

• **What did the crowds of people do?** (Some came to believe in Jesus.)

• **What good things can you do to get the word out about our church (or church club)?**

BIBLE BLUEPRINT MEMORY VERSE

Things You'll Need: Verse box (see Spice Box Project directions on p. 39), a Bible, copy of the verse words on different shapes of paper that have been cut apart, duct tape, masking tape, and scissors

"I will praise you, O Lord, with all my heart; I will tell of all your wonders."
Psalm 9:1 (NIV)

Put the verse pieces in the Bible. Then put the Bible in the box you used during last week's session. Tape the lid on with duct tape.

I have my verse box with me again today. It has this week's verse inside. What do you think I'm going to need to get inside of it this time? Allow children to guess. **That's right, I'm going to need my scissors.** Cut duct tape off and invite a child to open the lid. **Oh, my! Someone else has been using my scissors.** Hold up verse pieces. **Was it you?** Point to a child. **You?** Point to another child. **Hmmm! I guess now I'm going to need some help putting this verse together.** Tape all verse words up on the wall or on a chalkboard. **Now, let's see if we can put the verse words in the right order.** Invite children to guess which word comes first, second, and so on. When the verse words are in the correct order, have the group read the verse with you. Another option might be to tape the verse words onto the backs of different children. The kids in the audience might enjoy watching the children with the verse words being shuffled around as the verse is put together in the correct order.

What are some of God's wonders that we can tell others about? How could this make them interested in coming to church? Allow children to respond. Answers might include: to hear more about God, to be with other people who are interested in learning about God, and so on.

Younger children may learn a shortened version of the verse. Have them add actions such as:

I will tell (Hold hand up to mouth as if shouting.)

Of all (Spread arms out wide to the side.)

Your wonders. (Point up.)

Life Application
Small Group Time

Dismiss the children with their small group leaders, taking care to let the groups farthest away from the meeting area leave first. Each small group leader will need a copy of the Life Application Page for today. Be sure to give this page to leaders at least a week ahead of time so that they can be ready to work with their groups.

Children's Church Worship

Things You'll Need: *Bible Memory Toolbox* cassette, a cassette player, and an offering container

If you are using this section, be sure to allow kids a short time to stand up and stretch in between activities. You might also want to include some active songs during the singing time.

SINGING

Choose music that correlates with this week's On-the-Job Training Topic (Get the word out to your friends) and the Action Step (Say good things about your church). To reinforce this week's Bible Blueprint Verse, teach "I Will Praise You, O Lord" from page 119 of this book (also found on the *Bible Memory Toolbox* sing-along cassette tape).

CRITTER COUNTY STORY

Through the familiar and friendly Critter County characters, the children can see this week's theme in action and be motivated to get the word out by saying good things about their church. This week's story begins on page 65.

OFFERING

One way children can learn to worship and respond to God is by giving. If you are using this curriculum for a children's church program, you may prefer to take the offering now instead of during the Weekly Activities portion of the Bible Story Time. Encourage children to thank God for something either verbally or silently as the offering plate passes by.

PRAISE AND PRAYER

Continue to help children through a prayer experience by offering them a line and asking them to repeat it. (Refer to Session 1, p. 56.) This week, encourage children to think of someone they would like to tell about God and invite to church. Let the children conclude the prayer time with their own sentences, asking God to help them reach out to the person of their choice.

Midweek Extras

Things You'll Need: Masking tape, a cassette player, and the *Bible Memory Toolbox* cassette

If you are using this curriculum for a midweek children's program or as a combined Sunday School/Children's Church program during the Adventure, you may wish to add these fun activities to your time together.

GAME
Get the Good Word Out

Make sure there are no protruding or sharp objects that might cause a problem should a running child fall in the game area. Then, with masking tape mark two lines on opposite sides of the room. Have everyone line up on one side of the room, except for one person who stands in the middle of both lines. He or she is the caller who announces to everyone, "Get the good word out!" at which time everyone tries to run across the room without being tagged by the caller.

Anyone who is tagged by the caller must immediately be prepared to shout the name of someone they could talk to about church or church club. This person must be a real person who can be further identified if challenged. Example, "Who is Lois?" Answer, "My next door neighbor." The object is to get kids thinking about who they might get the word out to while having fun.

Adjustment for Younger Ages

Have children run with a partner or have them hop, crawl, or walk fast instead of running while playing the game.

SINGING

Singing is a fun way to praise God. Make use of the songs included in this book, beginning on page 119. The songs in this book are also found on the *Bible Memory Toolbox* sing-along cassette tape. Be sure to learn the song "I Will Praise You, Oh Lord" based on this week's Bible Blueprint Verse. And remember to include some active songs to give kids an opportunity to move around.

CRITTER COUNTY STORY

A Help in Trouble

(Ring a bell.) The church bell sounded and could be heard all over Critter County. Everyone from the church knew that someone was in danger or there was trouble somewhere in the county. The ducks waddled as quickly as they could, the elephants and big cats lumbered to the center of town, and the monkeys swung from branch to branch taking bunches of bananas with them.

"What's the matter? Is there a fire? Is someone hurt?" shouted the critters as they gathered 'round the flagpole in the courtyard. Pastor Penguin stepped up and said loudly, "Everyone hurry. We have a major emergency. Oscar Ostrich, a new critter in our town, went out into the woods early this morning to pick blackberries, and he has not returned for his appointment with Dr. Duck. We KNOW something has happened to him, and we have to find him."

All the ostriches, kittens, frogs, and other critters from the church moved forward toward Pastor Penguin so they could learn how they could help. Pastor Penguin divided all the critters into groups of four or five and asked one of the adult critters to be in charge of each group. Quickly they split up and headed for the Critter County woods to search for Oscar.

The second group that headed toward the woods had Motorboat the beaver, Lunchbox the lion cub, and Okey Dokey the donkey in it. Sydney the squirrel had offered to head up this group of critters. As they started toward the woods and were getting close to Heartbreak Hill, Lunchbox leaned over to Motorboat and whispered, "I can't believe we got stuck with Okey Dokey. He's so slow, we'll never find Oscar going at this pace."

"Yeah, and his ears are so long and droopy that I'll trip over them if I'm not careful," chimed in Motorboat. Fortunately, neither Sydney nor Okey Dokey heard Lunchbox and Motorboat talking about Okey Dokey like that.

All the groups looked and looked for the missing ostrich. No one could find him. They looked all over Heartbreak Hill, they searched all through the apple orchard, and they climbed trees so they could see down the valley. Everyone was getting tired and discouraged. Night was falling like a big blanket over Critter County, and many critters were discussing whether or not they could continue searching. Just about the time all hope of finding Oscar was nearly lost, Okey Dokey said, "Shhh, I think I hear something!"

Sydney was smart enough to listen to what the young donkey had to say. "What do you hear?" he asked.

"Well, I can't be sure, but I think I heard what sounded like an Ostrich yelling for help."

"Shhhh, everybody be real quiet. Okey Dokey thinks he hears Oscar," said Sydney.

It got quiet and sure enough, Okey listened and listened with those big droopy ears. Then he led the group right over the creek to a little island filled with blackberry bushes. And there, lying on the ground, was Oscar.

"What happened? Are you hurt?" everyone asked at once.

Oscar grabbed his long left leg and moaned. He explained that he was trying to reach some of the berries on the top of the bush and had lost his balance.

"How are we going to get him back to Dr. Duck's office?" asked Motorboat.

"Well, if you all think it would be a good idea, we could make a sled-like stretcher for him. Then you could attach it to me. I walk so slowly that he would be very comfortable," offered Okey Dokey.

And that's exactly what they did. Soon they met up with the other groups that had been looking for Oscar. And everybody was glad they had found him.

On the way to Dr. Duck's, Oscar spoke to Pastor Penguin. "I don't know what I would have done without you and your kind friends. Thank you for helping me out."

"Oh, you're welcome, Oscar. The Critter County church folks are always glad to help others. In fact, some of the critters have already offered to come by and check on you from time to time. Would that be OK?"

"That would be great," answered Oscar. "And when I get better, I might do some checking myself."

"What's that?" asked Pastor Penguin.

"I'd like to come by and check out your church sometime. It must be a great place to have so many kind folks in it," said Oscar.

"It is, Oscar, it is," answered Pastor Penguin. "We'll look forward to your visit."

Life Application Page

For Small Group Leaders

▶ **WEEK TWO** ◀

ON-THE-JOB TRAINING TOPIC:

Get the word out to your friends

ACTION STEP:

Say good things about your church

BIBLE STORY:

Acts 5:12–16

MEMORY VERSE:

Psalm 9:1 (NIV)

THINGS YOU'LL NEED:

- Copy of "Tips for Small Group Leaders" from pages 23–24
- Action Step/Training Topic poster (made in advance)
- Children's Journal
- Adventure Prayer poster (made in advance)
- Children's Activity Book
- Poster board
- Markers
- Chalkboard and chalk

IN ADVANCE:

Make a tool-shaped poster of the Adventure Prayer on page 24. Also make tool-shaped posters of the Action Step and On-the-Job Training Topic.

KID TALK

This is an important time for children to talk with one another about who they would like to invite to church. It's also a good opportunity to share positive things about the church and discuss ways to let other people know about those things. Use these questions to get the group talking.

• **Who are some people you might feel comfortable talking to about our church (or church club)? What could you say?**

• **In our Bible story today, how did Jesus' followers get the word out?** (By doing good things for people)

• **What are some things our church (or church club) does that would interest people?** (Answers might include: helping people who need food or clothes, having Christian music concerts, having Vacation Bible School, and so on.) **Do you have any other ideas of things we could do?**

Show Action Step and Training posters for this week. **This week's On-the-Job-Training Topic is "Get the word out to your friends." One way we do that is by practicing this week's Action Step. It is, "Say good things about your church." We do that to help interest people in our church. The church is a great place to learn more about God and find out what it's like to be a part of his family. God can't do that without people like you and me becoming friends with people who need to know about Jesus.**

We talked earlier about the kinds of things we could tell others about our church. Are there any other good things we could tell them about our church (or church club)? Use a large poster board that you can design and leave up for the rest of the Adventure. Encourage children to think of everything they can, from worship services to nursery care, a beautiful choir, a nice building, a great pastor, terrific teachers, friends to learn with, programs offered by your church, and so on. If you have time, let your group decorate the poster as you celebrate all the wonderful things your church has to offer.

Did anyone do something special to care for someone last week? Let children respond. Celebrate any good deeds and praise students for carrying out the Action Step from last week. **Now I have two questions for those of you who are working in your journals. Who did you pick as the most loving person you know, and why did you pick him or her?** If time permits, allow children who don't have journals to talk about a loving person they know, too.

PRAYER TALK

When we talk to God today, let's mention the people we want to share his Word with. Let's start by praying our Adventure Prayer and finish by celebrating something good about our church!

Using the Adventure Prayer poster, read the prayer together with your group. Encourage kids to conclude by saying something good about their church and telling God someone they would like to share that with. Be sure to ask the group about any special prayer concerns or requests, and end by praying for each one.

Small Group Tip

Children will open up more with you and with each other as they get to know you better and realize that what they have to say is important. Take time to call each child by name. Record special notes about each child in a journal so that you can have a reflection sheet to refer to before you begin your small group time each week. Children will appreciate that you took time out to remember their special needs. You will build a foundation of trust and friendship and will open the door to meaningful communication.

WEEK three

▶ **OVERVIEW** ◀

On-the-Job Training Topic: Open the door
Action Step: Be caring and make a new friend
Bible Story: Acts 10:1–35
Memory Verse: Acts 10:35 (ICB)

GETTING STARTED

As the children arrive, they should stop by the Adventure check-in table to record their attendance, pick up their color-coded name tags, and meet their small group leaders. They can then proceed to work on the Bible-time project of their choice or move to the Bible Story Time with their small group leaders.

 Bible-Time Projects

Continue to offer ongoing projects, adding new ones as your schedule permits. Consider any new projects that correlate with this week's lesson.

 Bible Story Time

Gather the children together in a large group with their small group leaders.

WEEKLY ACTIVITIES

Welcome the children back to the Adventure. Proceed by making any necessary announcements, recognizing birthdays, or taking an offering. Remember not to spend too much time here so that your story presentation will not be rushed.

SETTING THE SCENE

Things You'll Need: Safety cones, construction worker clothes (an orange safety vest, work boots, hardhat [may be purchased at a party store], and jeans), hammer, nails, paint and brushes, a sawhorse, a piece of flat wood and the wooden Training Notice Post you used in Week 1, a construction boot, a copy of the Action Step, a chair, and an old doorknob

Preparation

Make the area look like a construction site, and dress in your construction crew work gear. Paint this week's On-the-Job Training Topic on a piece of wood. Make it large enough for kids to read. Put the wood out of sight behind a door. Place a copy of this week's Action Step in the boot. Place the boot by the Training Notice Post. Then tuck the old doorknob in a back pocket.

Topic Introduction

Well, hello! How are all my construction workers doing? Allow kids to respond. **That's great. I hope you're all ready to learn more about how to build a church where everyone can feel loved and welcomed. But before we go on to this week's Training Topic, who can read the two topics we've already covered from our Training Notice Post?** Have a child read the two topics. **Did anybody talk to someone about church (or church club) this week?** Have kids raise hands. **Did anybody do something kind for someone this week?**

Have kids raise their hands. **Good job! Now, it's time for this week's On-the-Job Training Topic.** Scratch head. **But I can't remember where I put our sign. Hmmm! And I brought something with me to help me remember where I put it, too. And now I can't remember what I brought with me to help me remember.** Turn around as you are thinking so kids can see the big bulge in your pocket. **Maybe if I sit down it'll help me think.** As soon as you sit down, jump up with a yell. **What was that?** Reach around to your back pocket and pull out the doorknob. **Now, how did that get there? Oh, I remember! I brought this door knob to remind me where I put the Training Topic for today.** Walk over and get topic from behind the door. Show it to kids. **Well, what do you know! It says, "Open the door."** Have a child assist in nailing it on the post. **What kind of door do you think this is talking about?** Allow for children to respond. **God wants us to open the doors of our hearts and our church to people who are new to our area and to those who might be feeling left out or different. But how do we do that? Let's see what our Action Step tells us to do.** Have someone come up and take the Action Step out of the work boot. Read it to the group. **It says, "Be caring and make a new friend." Today's Bible story is about how Peter made a new friend. Maybe it will help us discover how we can do this, too. Let's watch.**

BIBLE STORY PRESENTATION

Bible Basis: *Acts 10:1–35*
Character: *Cornelius*

Things You'll Need: Bible-time clothing. (This could be made in Weeks 1 and 2 in the Bible-time costume project.)

Today's story is a monologue by Cornelius. Cornelius was a Gentile and a centurion. In the Roman legions, centurions commanded a "century" of 100 soldiers. Centurions were carefully selected men of noble qualities, essential to the stability of the Roman government. Cornelius was a devout and God-fearing man who believed in one God and respected the moral and ethical teaching of the Jews. He did not, however, have faith in Christ. Cornelius should tell this story as his own. He should make every attempt to learn the story and explain the events, rather than read a script. It will be much more meaningful for the listeners!

Hello. I was just listening to your talk about opening doors and making new friends. By the way, my name is Cornelius, and I have a story to share with you about opening doors and making new friends. I'm a centurion. That means that I work for the Roman government and oversee what you would call a military unit. My family and I are God-fearing people. We worship and pray regularly. We do all we can to help the poor and needy. I imagine we're a lot like many of you.

One day at three in the afternoon—that's our time of prayer—I had a vision. Now, this was no ordinary vision. And it wasn't a dream or a figment of my imagination either. It was an angel of God who came to me and called me by name.

"Cornelius!" he called. Now, you can imagine how frightened I was! This wasn't a daily occurrence, you know. I swallowed hard and bravely asked, "What is it, Lord?"

The angel told me that my prayers and gifts to the poor had been accepted as an offering before God. Then the angel went on to tell me that I was to send some men to a place called Joppa and have them bring back a man named Peter. He was staying at a house by the sea. I didn't know why the angel of

God told me to do this, but I wasn't going to question him. I did just as I was told. I called two of my servants and one of my soldiers who also believed in God and told them everything that had happened. Then I sent them to Joppa to bring Peter to my home. I can't tell you how curious I was to know what this was all about! I was worried that Peter would not come. Not only was I a stranger to Peter, but he was a Jew and I was a Gentile! Jews and Gentiles did not associate with one another. But I'll come back to that in just a moment.

Later I found out that Peter had had a vision from God, too. During Peter's vision he saw a sheet being let down to earth by four corners. It contained all sorts of four-footed animals, reptiles, and birds. Then a voice told him, "Get up, Peter. Kill and eat." Well, Peter was confused because that went against the Jewish food laws. God had given these laws in the Old Testament. And in them God had told the Jewish people things they could and could not eat. Every animal Peter saw in the sheet was an animal that God had told the Jews NOT to use for food. So he responded by saying, "Surely not, Lord! I have never eaten anything impure or unclean." Well, the voice spoke to him a second time and told him, "Do not call anything impure that God has made clean." You see, God wasn't just talking about meat. But I'm getting ahead of myself. Peter saw the vision three times.

While all this was taking place, my men found Simon's house. That's where Peter was staying. As my men approached the house the Holy Spirit spoke to Peter once more. He said, "Three men are looking for you. Get up and go downstairs. Do not hesitate to go with them, for I have sent them." So Peter came down to tell my men that he was the one they were looking for, and then he asked them why they had come. My men told him the whole story about my vision, and Peter graciously invited them in, despite the fact that they were Gentiles. And then he provided lodging for them because it was too late in the day to return to Caesarea, where I live.

The next day I called together all of my relatives and close friends, hoping that my men would return home with Peter. And they did. I invited Peter into my home, and we all awaited what he had to say to us. He spoke, "You all know that it is against our law for a Jew to associate with a Gentile or visit him. But God has shown me that I should not call any man impure or unclean. So when I was sent for, I came." You see, in Peter's vision God was helping Peter understand that all people are valuable to God. It doesn't matter what people look like, how they talk, or what country they come from.

Peter continued, "I now realize how true it is that God does not show favoritism, but accepts people from every nation who fear him and do what is right." Peter's words were true. God loves everyone, and he wants us to do the same. He wants us to open our hearts and our churches to new people. We all have a lot to learn from each other. That's what Peter and I found out that day. And the best part was that Peter told us about Jesus and we became Christians. What a wonderful gift Peter gave to us! And all because he was willing to open the doors of his heart to new friends. I hope you will be willing to open your heart and make a new friend, too!

COMPREHENSION QUESTIONS

Briefly discuss these questions with the children to clarify the main ideas in the Bible story presentation.

• **What was the barrier or closed door between Cornelius and Peter?** (Cornelius was a Gentile [anyone who is not Jewish] and Peter was a Jew. Jews and Gentiles were not friendly with one another.)

• **What was similar about both Cornelius and Peter?** (They both believed in God. And they were both willing to listen to God when he spoke to them in their visions.)

• **Who made a new friend?** (Both Cornelius and Peter.)

• **How did they become friends?** (Cornelius invited Peter to his house. Peter came and told Cornelius and his family and friends about Jesus.)

BIBLE BLUEPRINT MEMORY VERSE

Things You'll Need: Verse box with lid bolted on, a wrench, a Bible, and a copy of this week's verse

"God accepts anyone who worships him and does what is right. It is not important what country a person comes from." Acts 10:35 (ICB)

You will need today's memory verse written on a large piece of paper. Fold it and put it in a Bible. Place the Bible inside the verse box and bolt the box shut. If you have someone in your congregation who speaks another language, consider having the person teach your group how to say or write the verse in his or her language.

It seems that my verse box isn't going to open like it did last week. I'm going to need another tool. Anybody know which one? Allow kids to respond. **Hey! That's a great idea. Let's try opening the lid by using my wrench to loosen the bolt.** Loosen the bolt. Invite someone to take off the lid. Pull out the Bible memory verse for the day. Ask one of the children to read the first sentence.

"God accepts anyone who worships him and does what is right." Who does this verse say is accepted by God? Allow kids to respond. **That's a lot of people. The verse also says, "It is not important what country a person comes from." What do you think God means by that?** Allow kids to respond. If you have invited a guest to share the verse, have him or her come up at this time and teach the verse in another language.

Younger children can learn a shortened version of the verse: "God accepts anyone who worships him and does what is right." End this section today by reminding children that even if we can't speak another person's language, we can do kind things for him or her. Kindness is a language that everyone understands.

Life Application
Small Group Time

Dismiss the children with their small group leaders, taking care to let the groups farthest away from the meeting area leave first. Each small group leader will need a copy of the Life Application Page for today. Be sure to give this page to leaders at least a week ahead of time so that they can be ready to work with their groups.

Children's Church Worship

Things You'll Need: *Bible Memory Toolbox* cassette, a cassette player, and an offering container

If you are using this section, be sure to allow kids a short time to stand up and stretch in between activities. You might also want to include some active songs during the singing time.

SINGING

Choose music that correlates with this week's On-the-Job Training Topic (Open the door) and the Action Step (Be caring and make a new friend). To reinforce this week's verse, teach "God Accepts Anyone" from page 120 of this book (also found on the *Bible Memory Toolbox* sing-along cassette tape).

CRITTER COUNTY STORY

Through the familiar and friendly Critter County characters, the children can see this week's theme in action and be motivated to open the door to others and make new friends. This week's story begins on page 74.

OFFERING

Provide the children an opportunity to respond to God by giving. If you are using this curriculum for a children's church program, you may prefer to take the offering now instead of during Weekly Activities at the start of the Bible Story Time. Encourage children to thank God for something either verbally or silently as the offering plate passes by.

PRAISE AND PRAYER

Continue to help children through a prayer experience by saying one line of a prayer and asking them to repeat it. This week, encourage children to open a door of friendship and meet someone new. Let the children conclude the prayer time with their own sentences asking God to help them to make new friends.

 **Midweek Extras**

Things You'll Need: Golf balls, child-sized golf clubs or hockey sticks, poster board, markers, scissors, a cassette player, and the *Bible Memory Toolbox* cassette

If you are using this curriculum for a midweek children's program or as a combined Sunday School/Children's Church program during the Adventure, you may wish to add these fun activities to your time together.

GAME

Through the Door

Divide the children into small groups of three. Make sure you have an older child who can cut the poster board in each group. Ask the children to think of different doors they must go through to meet people. List them. (Examples: store doors, home doors, airplane doors, "doors" to different countries, school doors, and so on.) Give each small group a piece of sturdy poster board, markers, and

scissors. Have them design a golf-ball size "door" by cutting a hole or "door" large enough for a golf ball to get through in the bottom of the poster board. (Make the actual holes larger than the size of a golf ball for greater ease in playing the game.) Then have kids decorate their poster boards. Fold each piece of poster board so that it will stand up and so the doorway (for the ball) will allow kids to hit their balls through. Place the doorways at various locations around the room and let students enjoy sending the golf balls through the open doors. (Make sure that when you set up the "golf course" you place it where children will be able to play safely.) This activity works best on a carpeted surface where the balls will not roll out of control. Also have children tap balls gently to avoid hitting anyone with a flying golf ball.

Adjustment for Younger Ages

Cut golf game doors in advance.

SINGING

Singing is a fun way to praise God. Make use of the songs included in this book, beginning on page 119. The songs in this book are also found on the *Bible Memory Toolbox* sing-along cassette tape. Be sure to learn the song "God Accepts Anyone" based on this week's Bible verse. And remember to include some active songs to give kids an opportunity to move around.

CRITTER COUNTY STORY

A Skunk of a Different Color

It was one of those spring afternoons that everyone enjoys. The birds sang perfectly in tune and the butterflies moved freely from blossom to blossom. High, puffy clouds moved in front of the sun from time to time, providing shade for the critters playing soccer in the park. It was the best of times for everyone but Cocoa the skunk.

The little brown skunk had arrived on the outskirts of Critter County after a long and difficult trip. Her backpack had grown heavy and her paws sore because the road had been so long. But memories of the nasty names she had been called, "Brownie," and "Ugly," kept pushing her toward Critter County. She had heard of this place from her cousins. It promised to be a shelter and a safe place for her. She hoped that no one there would call her ugly names because she was different from most skunks who are black with a white stripe. Where does a brown skunk with no stripe go to fit in? Perhaps to Critter County.

For Critter County is known throughout the land as a place where all are loved and accepted . . . no matter what they look like, how smart they are, or how well they play sports. Surely Cocoa would find a new home.

Her arrival in town was quiet.

As she neared the center of the town, Sydney the squirrel spotted her. "Well, hello, there. I don't believe I've had the pleasure of your acquaintance before," he said with his cutest squirrel giggle. "What's your name?"

"Well, my name is Cocoa," she said as she tucked her head into her shoulder. She was afraid that when she spoke and Sydney realized she was a brown skunk, he would laugh like everyone else had always done. But he didn't!

"That's a perfect name for a beautiful brown skunk like you!"

"I never thought of it that way," said Cocoa.

"Come on, Miss Cocoa, I'll take you over to the school and introduce you to some friends," offered Sydney.

"No, thank you. I had better just stay by myself," answered Cocoa.

Several days passed and Sydney could not stop thinking about the shy brown skunk. *I think I'll try to find her after I brush my teeth and tail*, he thought to himself.

A stroll through the Critter County park found Cocoa sitting on a swing. Her tail was blowing back and forth in the breeze. "Hi, there, Cocoa; it's good to see you again," shouted Sydney from the apple tree.

"Hi, Sydney. How are you?" she answered.

Sydney was encouraged by her response. However, his little squirrel heart was sad when he got close enough to see her face. "Why, Cocoa, you don't look very happy. Is there anything I can do to help you?"

"I am just so tired of always playing by myself," Cocoa said as she began to cry.

Sydney figured out that she had probably been teased a lot in her lifetime and that she had grown very much afraid of attempting to make new friends. So he decided to try and help.

"Cocoa, I'm having some kids up to my tree house tonight for homemade acorn ice cream, and I could sure use some help getting ready and then serving. Would you be available to help me?"

Cocoa thought for a few minutes and finally said, "Yes, I can come and help you, Sydney."

They set the time and he gave her directions to get to his house.

The clever little squirrel with the big heart smiled all the way home at the thought of Cocoa meeting so many of the Critter County kids that night. He knew down deep in his heart that Cocoa would make lots of new friends who would like her as much as he did. And he was right.

From that evening on, Miss Cocoa had many friends. You see, the critters in this county have learned to look not just at the way someone appears on the outside, but to look deep inside. Often the kindest, most loving hearts are inside those who may look a little different from you.

Life Application Page

For Small Group Leaders

▶ **WEEK THREE** ◀

ON-THE-JOB TRAINING TOPIC:
Open the door

ACTION STEP:
Be caring and make a new friend

BIBLE STORY:
Acts 10:1–35

MEMORY VERSE:
Acts 10:35 (ICB)

THINGS YOU'LL NEED:

- Copy of "Tips for Small Group Leaders" from pages 23–24
- Action Step/Training Topic poster (made in advance)
- Children's Journal
- Slips of paper
- A brown paper bag
- Adventure Prayer poster (made in advance)
- Children's Activity Book

IN ADVANCE:

Make a tool-shaped poster of the Adventure Prayer on page 24. Also make tool-shaped posters of the Action Step and On-the-Job Training Topic.

KID TALK

One of the Action Steps or goals of this session is to encourage children to make new friends. If your group members do not know one another very well, this is a good chance to ask young people to open up more about themselves. Invite kids to share some of their likes, dislikes, hobbies, and special interests. Use these questions to further your discussion.

- **Is it easy or difficult to talk to someone that you don't know very well? Why?**
- **Why is knowing people who are different from us a good thing?** (We can learn things from them, they can learn things from us, it helps us to see people in a new way, and so on.)
- **In our Bible story today, how did Peter and Cornelius become friends?** (Cornelius invited Peter to his house. Peter came and talked about Jesus.)
- **What are some qualities of a good friend? Which of those qualities do you feel you have to offer someone?**

- **Can you name one or two people you would like to get to know better and make friends with?** (Let children make as many suggestions as they can come up with.)

Then ask: **Did anyone have a chance to share something good about their church with someone? Did anyone invite someone new to church this week?** Let children respond. Celebrate what the children have done. **And for those of you working in your journals, here is your question: "What four things can we do to help others?"** (Listen, pray, love, and share.) Point to the On-the-Job Training Topic and Action Step posters. **Today's Training Topic is "Open the door." The Action Step is "Be caring and make a new friend." Let's think about these as we pray today.**

PRAYER TALK

Let's start our prayer by using the Adventure Prayer. At the end of our

prayer, let's ask for God's help in making new friends with some of the people we talked about.

Use the Adventure Prayer poster, reading it together with your group. Close the prayer time by asking for God's help in opening your hearts to meeting new people and making new friends. Don't forget to include any special prayer concerns or requests the children may have.

Small Group Tip

You are now three weeks into the process of getting to know one another. This is a good time to have everyone in the group write down their name on a small piece of paper and place it into a brown paper bag. Pass the bag around the room. Have each child draw one name out of the bag as it is passed. Be sure that no one obtains his or her own name. Tell the group that they have just drawn the name of their prayer partner. Children should remember to pray for their partner this week. This is a great way to encourage students to start thinking about and caring for another person. The children will also feel good knowing that someone new will be praying for them this week!

▶ **OVERVIEW** ◀

On-the-Job Training Topic: Use your tools well

Action Step: Put your talents to use

Bible Story: Acts 18:24–28

Memory Verse: 1 Peter 4:10a (NIV)

GETTING STARTED

As the children arrive, they should stop by the Adventure check-in table to record their attendance, pick up their color-coded name tags, and meet their small group leaders. They can then proceed to work on the Bible-time project of their choice or move to the Bible Story Time with their small group leaders.

 Bible-Time Projects

Continue to offer ongoing projects, adding new ones as your schedule permits. Consider any new projects that correlate with this week's lesson.

 Bible Story Time

Gather the children together in a large group with their small group leaders.

WEEKLY ACTIVITIES

Welcome the children back to the Adventure. Proceed by making any necessary announcements, recognizing birthdays, or taking an offering. Remember not to spend too much time here so that your story presentation will not be rushed.

SETTING THE SCENE

Things You'll Need: Safety cones, construction worker clothes (an orange safety vest, work boots, hardhat [may be purchased at a party store], and jeans), hammer, nails, paint

and brushes, a sawhorse, a piece of flat wood and the wooden Training Notice Post you used last week, a construction boot, a copy of the Action Step, and a toolbox with "talent labels" on each of the tools

Preparation

Make the area look like a construction site, and dress in your construction crew work gear. Paint this week's On-the-Job Training Topic on a piece of wood. Make it large enough for kids to read. Tuck a copy of this week's Action Step in the boot. Place the boot by the Training Notice Post. Tape one of these labels on each of the tools in the toolbox: sings well; good at sports; a good friend; explains things well; helps others; a good speaker; strong; good at fixing things; good problem solver; doesn't give up easily; and so on. Then put tools into the toolbox. Set the toolbox within arm's reach.

Topic Introduction

Hello! It's great to see all of you back again! We've come a long way in building a place where everyone can feel loved and welcomed, don't you think? We've learned how to take care of each other, get the word out about our church, and open the door to new friendships! I'm pretty excited about this week's lesson, too. It's about

using our tools well. **Each one of us has special tools that God has given us. Does anybody know what those tools might be?** Invite children to give their answers. **Well, well, you gave some good answers, but let's look inside our toolbox and see what tools we have in here.** Invite children one at a time to come up and get a tool out of the toolbox. Have him or her read the label on the tool. **Wow! What a lot of tools! Our tools are our talents. And looking out at all of you . . . whew! What an enormous sea of talent! Let's take a moment to put up this week's Training Topic and dig out the Action Step that goes with it.** Have a child assist you as you nail up this week's topic, "Use your tools well." Then have another child come up and pull out the Action Step, "Put your talents to use." **"Put your talents to use." I wonder what that means? Well, it's time for the Bible story now. Today's story . . .** Leader is interrupted by loud humming of girl puppet. Leader sits down quietly as Kitty begins.

BIBLE STORY PRESENTATION

Bible Basis: *Acts 18:24–28*
Characters: *Two kids, Kitty and*
                     Donald
Things You'll Need: *A boy and a girl puppet*
                     Lots of paper scraps

Today's story is told through a puppet presentation. If you do not have a boy and a girl puppet, make simple puppets out of socks or paper bags. If you do not have a puppet stage, simply drape a curtain around a folding table, and

ask your puppeteers to kneel beneath the curtained table. At the start of the scene the puppet stage is covered with paper scraps. **Kitty** *is humming very loudly and pretending to tear up more paper scraps.*

Kitty: I just love tearing up paper bits to make mosaic pictures. [*To the kids in audience*] Have you ever made a mosaic picture? [*Enter Donald.*]

Donald: Kitty, what in the world are you doing?

Kitty: Tearing up paper scraps for my new mosaic.

Donald: It looks like you have enough paper there for ten mosaics. By the way, why are you making a mosaic?

Kitty: Because I have a talent for making mosaics. And I heard Leader's Name say that we should use our talents to help others.

Donald: When did you hear her (or him) say that?

Kitty: Well, Leader's Name was practicing telling today's Bible story so he (or she) would be ready for all the Adventure kids here at Name of time you are using this program, such as Children's Church.

Donald: Ooooo. I love Bible stories. What was the Bible story about?

Kitty: A gorilla.

Donald: A gorilla? I don't remember any Bible stories about a gorilla.

Kitty: Sure it was. It was about someone named Priscilla and her husband the gorilla. I remember because that rhymes.

Donald: Where was the story from?

Kitty: Um, Acts 18, I think.

Donald: Wait just a minute. I'll go look it up in my Bible. [*Donald goes out of a sight then reappears.*]

Donald: I think you meant Priscilla and Aquila.

Kitty: Oh, you're right. It was Priscilla and Aquila.

Donald: And there was another man named Apollos.

Kitty: That's right. Apollos's talent was that he was a good speaker. And he used his talent to teach others about God. There was a problem, though.

Donald: What was that?

Kitty: Apollos was a good speaker, but he needed someone to teach him more about God. There were lots of things that he didn't know.

Donald: Sounds like he needed to find someone who had the talent for teaching and explaining things.

Kitty: I'm getting to that part. One day when he was speaking in the synagogue, there were two people named Priscilla and Gorilla—I mean, Aquila—who heard him. Priscilla and Aquila invited Apollos to their home. While he was there, they helped Apollos learn more about God and Jesus so he could be an even better speaker.

Donald: That was very nice of them.

Kitty: They knew that Apollos had a special talent for speaking and sharing God's Word with others. So they wanted to help him learn how to use his talents well.

Donald: By teaching him more about Jesus!

Kitty: That's right. And when Apollos wanted to go to a place called Achaia to spread God's Word, Priscilla and Aquila encouraged him to go. Why, they even wrote to the disciples in Achaia and told them Apollos was coming.

Donald: What a great idea. Sounds like they had a talent for encouraging people, too. What a good story. But it makes me kind of sad.

Kitty: Why?

Donald: I don't know if I have any talents.

Kitty: Oh, sure you do! God gave everyone talent tools to use to help others. Let's go get some cookies and maybe I can help you figure out what your talents are.

Donald: Is eating cookies a talent?

Kitty: I don't think so, but we'll talk about it. Come on! [*Puppets exit.*]

Leader: Well, I guess I don't need to tell you the Bible story I had been practicing. Kitty did a good job. One of her talents must be having a good memory! Now let's talk about the story.

COMPREHENSION QUESTIONS

Briefly discuss these questions with the children to clarify the main ideas in the Bible story presentation.

• **Who had a talent for speaking?** (Apollos)

• **Who recognized this special talent in Apollos?** (Priscilla and Aquila.)

• **What talents did Priscilla and Aquila have?** (Encouraging others and knowing how to explain and teach things about God.)

• **What did they do for Apollos?** (They taught him about Jesus and encouraged Apollos to go to Achaia to spread God's Word.)

BIBLE BLUEPRINT MEMORY VERSE

Things You'll Need: Verse box with lid nailed on, a hammer, a Bible, the verse written on a small piece of paper, and a small gift-wrapped box

"Each one should use whatever gift he has received to serve others."
1 Peter 4:10a (NIV)

Today put the verse in the small box and gift wrap it. Put the box under the Bible inside the verse box. When you nail the lid on, leave the nail heads sticking up. Lay a hammer nearby.

My verse box is really shut tight today! Looks like I'm going to need my hammer to get inside. Proceed to loosen the nails and pry open the box. You might want to invite a child up to help. **Now I can take out my Bible and see what our Bible Blueprint Verse is today.** Take out the Bible and look through it as if searching for the verse. **Why, that's funny. I can't seem to find the verse.** Look back into verse box. **Hmmm. I wonder if this has something to do with the verse?** Open the gift, then read the verse to the group. **"Each one should use whatever gift he has received to serve others" 1 Peter 4:10a.** Ask the group to repeat the verse with you. **Do you think the verse is talking about a gift like this?** Hold up gift box. **Or is it talking about something else?** Allow children to respond. **That's right. The gifts we receive from God are the talents and special abilities that each one of us has been blessed with. And God wants us to put those gifts to good use by serving others! Now, let's review the verse one more time**

with a chant. Divide the group into two parts, then teach kids this chant:

Group I:	Each one should use
Group II:	Who should use?
Group I:	Each one should use
Group II:	What should we use?
Group I:	Whatever gift
Group II:	What gift is that?
Group I:	The gift you have received
Group II:	Received from whom?
Group I:	Received from God
Group II:	And what should we do?
Group I:	Serve others with your gift.
Group II:	Serve others with our gift?
Group I and II:	Serve others with your gift. Yeah!

For younger children, if you have time you may wish to give everyone a piece of ribbon to tie around his or her wrist with the help of a partner. Explain that the ribbon will be a reminder to use gifts from God to serve others.

Life Application

Small Group Time

Dismiss the children to their small group leaders, taking care to let the groups farthest away from the meeting area leave first. Each small group leader will need a copy of the Life Application Page for today. Be sure to give this page to leaders at least a week ahead of time so that they can be ready to work with their groups.

Children's Church Worship

Things You'll Need: *Bible Memory Toolbox* cassette, cassette player, and an offering container

If you are using this section, be sure to allow

kids a short time to stand up and stretch in between activities. You might also want to include some active songs during the singing time.

SINGING

Choose music that correlates with this week's On-the-Job Training (Use your tools well) and the Action Step (Put your talents to use). To reinforce this week's Bible Blueprint Verse, teach "Use It!" from page 120 of this book (also found on the *Bible Memory Toolbox* sing-along cassette tape).

CRITTER COUNTY STORY

Through the familiar and friendly Critter County characters, the children can see this week's theme in action and be motivated to use their talents well. This week's story begins on page 83.

OFFERING

Provide the children an opportunity to respond to God by giving. If you are using this curriculum for a children's church program, you may prefer to take the offering now instead of during Weekly Activities at the start of the Bible Story Time. Encourage children to thank God for something either verbally or silently as the offering plate passes by.

PRAISE AND PRAYER

Continue to help children through a prayer experience by saying one line of a prayer and asking them to repeat it. Conclude the prayer by thanking God for all the special talents we have been blessed with. This week, encourage children to think of ways they can use their talents to help others.

Things You'll Need: A cassette player and the *Bible Memory Toolbox* cassette

If you are using this curriculum for a midweek children's program or as a combined Sunday School/Children's Church program during the Adventure, you may wish to add these fun activities to your time together.

GAME

Frozen Talent Tag

You will need a large, open area for this game. Since children will be running, make sure there are no protruding or sharp objects in the field of play. If you are playing outside, make sure the ground doesn't have any hidden holes that might cause a child to trip or fall. To start, set boundaries within which children may travel. Choose one person to be "it" at the start. Everyone else must run and try not to be tagged by the person who is "it."

When someone is tagged, he or she must pose in a position that portrays a specific talent and remain frozen in that position. Some examples include dancers, acrobats, athletes, singers, musicians, carpenters, writers, painters, and so on. Encourage children to use their imaginations! Other teammates must then try to unfreeze the tagged people by retagging them, or by pointing to the frozen person and guessing what talent he or she has modeled. After a few minutes of play, choose someone new to be "it" and resume the game. To make the game more challenging, don't let children pose for any one talent more than once.

Adjustment for Younger Ages

The game leader may need to give children who are tagged suggestions to as to how they could pose.

SINGING

Singing is a fun way to praise God. Make use of the songs included in this book, beginning on page 119. The songs in this book are also found on the *Bible Memory Toolbox* sing-along cassette tape. Be sure to learn the song "Use It!" based on this week's Bible Blueprint Verse. And remember to include some active songs to give kids an opportunity to move around.

CRITTER COUNTY STORY

Whoooo Is It?

It was one of the most distressing sounds ever heard. Late at night in Critter County, after most of the furry and feathered little friends had crawled into their nests for a cozy night's sleep, the moaning would begin.

"Whooooo. Whooooooooo. Whoooooooooo am I?"

Long after the full moon rose to just beyond the crooked old oak tree in the center of the Critter County park, the moaning would continue.

The penguin police had been called. The telephone operator had been asked. No one seemed to know what the sound was. Finally, everyone agreed that something had to be done. The babes in the Critter County nursery would hoot, baa, and chirp all night long because the wailing was keeping them all awake. Even Grandmother Mouse couldn't quiet them down in her comfortable rocking chair.

"OK, I'll do it," announced Sydney the squirrel at the emergency town meeting. "I'll stay up tonight and climb up and down the trees until I find out where the sound is coming from. I'll not rest; I'll not slumber until the mystery is solved!" he exclaimed.

So that very evening, Sydney drank his big mug–full of hazelnut flavored coffee to help keep him awake. After drinking the big cup of his high-powered coffee, the squirrel was wired for excitement. Sydney scampered up and down the apple and pear trees without even trying. He used the tree branches for a swing and shouted, "Wheeee," as he landed on the telephone wire above the post office. In fact, he was having so much fun, he almost forgot what he was doing!

Suddenly, from behind the old hen house, the sound started again and jarred the little squirrel back to reality. "Whoooo. Whooooooo. And again I say, whooooooo am I?" came the moans from high up in the elm tree. Sydney scampered up to the top faster than a pig can plop in a mud puddle. Suddenly, he spotted the noise maker just beyond a clump of leaves.

"Well, hello there," said Sydney in a cheery voice. "So you are our friend who has been calling out to us at night. What can we do for you, Mr. Owl?"

"My name is Oliver, but you can call me Ollie," said the owl as he stuck out his wing to shake Sydney's paw. "Nice to meet you."

"Likewise, I'm sure," said Sydney. "Why are you calling out all night, "Whoooo am I?"

"Well, seems like everybody else has a special job to do and special talents. The ducks have beautiful feathers that they leave all around. Then Poncho the pig collects them and stuffs them in pillows and sells them at his roadside stand. Lester the lion runs his gas station and his wife, Liona Lou, runs Lester. Everybody uses their talents each day. Then they gather around the dinner table with their families and eat some monkey chow or lion chow or whatever, and then they go to nest. And they sleep all night till Reilly the rooster wakes them up."

Sydney looked a little puzzled. "Yes, that's right. Why does that bother you?" he asked.

"Because I don't have a job and I'm not good at anything. I sleep all day while they are working, and I'm awake all night. Talk about having your wires crossed and being a misfit!" said Ollie with a tear in his eye.

Sydney raised up on his hind paws. "Tell you what, Ollie. I have an idea. I will meet you here tomorrow night, same time and same place. OK?"

The next afternoon the squirrel gathered all the town leaders together and explained the situation. He told them that poor Ollie was discouraged because he didn't think he had any talents. So all the critters put their heads together and their paws and wings into a circle. "We'll help him," they promised each other. And they did.

From that night on, Critter County had its own special watchman. Because Ollie was good at staying awake at night and he had good eyesight, he would be the perfect night watchman for the little town. Every night from then on Patrolman Oliver the Owl sat proudly on a perch in the old elm tree. His hat and uniform looked so dignified. And everyone in Critter County was happy to get a good and safe night's sleep.

Life Application Page

For Small Group Leaders

▶ WEEK FOUR ◀

ON-THE-JOB TRAINING TOPIC:

Use your tools well

ACTION STEP:

Put your talents to use

BIBLE STORY:

Acts 18:24–28

MEMORY VERSE:

1 Peter 4:10a (NIV)

THINGS YOU'LL NEED:

- Copy of "Tips for Small Group Leaders" from pages 23–24
- Action Step/Training Topic poster (made in advance)
- Children's Journal
- Adventure Prayer poster (made in advance)
- Children's Activity Book
- Newsprint
- Marker
- Chalkboard and chalk

IN ADVANCE:

Make a tool-shaped poster of the Adventure Prayer on page 24. Also make tool-shaped posters of the Action Step and On-the-Job Training Topic.

KID TALK

This week's On-the-Job Training Topic and Action Step focus on recognizing our God-given gifts and putting them to good use. Most younger children will enjoy identifying things they do well. Older children have a tendency to shy away from such admissions and will need your assistance and support to help acknowledge their gifts. Begin your discussion by asking students to identify traits in people they admire. List all responses. Ask them to explain their answers by sharing why they admire particular traits. Continue your discussion with the following questions.

- **What talents did the people in our Bible story have?** (Apollos had a talent for public speaking, Aquila and Priscilla had the talents of encouraging others and being able to teach about God's Word.)
- **How can you use your talents to do something for others?**
- **How can you use your talents to do something for God?**

- **Now ask the person on your right and your left what they think they are good at. Perhaps you could make a suggestion if your neighbor has a hard time coming up with something.** Allow time for children to talk to their neighbors. **What did you find out?** Take the time to list the special talents and abilities of each person in your group. Be sure to include everyone.
- **Who are some people who help others put their talents to use?** (Teachers, coaches, and so on.)
- **What can you do to help others put their talents to good use?**

Did anyone make an effort to meet someone new or make a new friend last week? Allow time for children to respond and describe what happened. **For those of you working in your journals, what good things about your church have you written down?**

PRAYER TALK

Today during our prayer time, think about something that you're really good at and want to put to good use. At the end of our Adventure Prayer, we'll take the time to let everyone thank God for his or her special gift. Use the Adventure Prayer poster, reading together with your group. Make time to include any special prayer concerns or requests the children may have.

Small Group Tip

As your group gets to know one another better, you will not only observe developing friendships, but you may also notice that several children are having trouble fitting in.

(If that's not the case, then celebrate the positive relationships being built in your group!) Be very sensitive to this. It's easy to focus on the joy of growing and working friendships. Take an inventory of what is being shared in your group. Has everyone had a chance to share his or her ideas and answers?

Because some students will be particularly cautious about opening up to others, you don't need to require everyone's participation in any given discussion. But you do want to look for opportunities for timid students to open up. When they do choose to speak, allow them time to expand on their answers by asking one or two follow-up questions as well. And let everyone know that their honest answers are appreciated and respected.

WEEK five

GETTING STARTED

As the children arrive, they should stop by the Adventure check-in table to record their attendance, pick up their color-coded name tags, and meet their small group leaders. They can then proceed to work on the Bible-time project of their choice or move to the Bible Story Time with their small group leaders.

 Bible-Time Projects

Continue to offer ongoing projects, adding new ones as your schedule permits. Consider any new projects that correlate with this week's lesson.

 Bible Story Time

Gather the children together in a large group with their small group leaders.

WEEKLY ACTIVITIES

Welcome the children back to the Adventure. Proceed by making any necessary announcements, recognizing birthdays, or taking an offering. Remember not to spend too much time here so that your story presentation will not be rushed.

SETTING THE SCENE

Things You'll Need: Safety cones, construction worker clothes (an orange safety vest, work boots, hardhat [may be purchased at a party store], and jeans), hammer, nails, paint and brushes, a sawhorse, a piece of flat wood and the wooden Training Notice Post you used in Week 1, a construction boot, a copy of the Action Step, and a broom and dustpan

Preparation

Make the area look like a construction site. Dress in your construction crew work gear. Paint this week's On-the-Job Training Topic on a piece of wood, making it large enough for kids to read, and tuck a copy of this week's Action Step in the boot. Place the boot by the Training Notice Post and have the broom and dustpan nearby. The dustpan should have a note on the back of it that says, "Clean things out." The leader should be sweeping with the broom as he or she starts talking to the children.

Topic Introduction

Why, hello! Everybody ready to work today? Who remembers what we learned last week about being one of God's construction workers? Allow kids to respond. **"Use your tools or talents well." That's right.** Start sweeping again as you talk. **Well, this week we're going to learn about another thing that all construction workers need to do from time to time.**

And that is to . . . um . . . that's funny. **I wrote down what we were going to be learning about somewhere.** Pick up dustpan so that kids can see the note but you can't. Move as if you're going to use the dustpan. **Now, where did I put that note to myself? Anybody see a note lying around here?** Allow kids to answer. **Oh, there it is.** Looking on the back of the dustpan, read the note. **It says, "Clean things out." That's what we're going to learn about today, cleaning things out. Hmmm. I wonder what kinds of things. Does anybody have any ideas?** Allow kids to answer. Answers might include bad habits and attitudes such as jealousy, saying mean things, being unfriendly to those not in our special group of friends, not wanting to come to church, and so on. **Those are all good answers. Let's put up our Training Topic.** Nail topic to Training Notice Post. **It says, "Take out the trash." And our Action Step says** (pull step out of boot), **"Clean up garbage thoughts and actions." Let's take a look at today's Bible story and see if it has anything to say about cleaning up garbage thoughts and actions.**

BIBLE STORY PRESENTATION

Bible Basis: Acts 20:32–38
                       Ephesians 4:26–32
Characters: Karen (modern-day woman)
                       Tony (modern-day man)
                       Bible-time friend 1
                       Bible-time friend 2

Things You'll Need: A Bible
                              Bible-time costumes
                                 for witnesses

Today's drama is an interaction between contemporary characters and friends of the apostle Paul who bid him farewell as he was leaving for a journey. If you are short on actors, the roles of Karen and Tony can be read by one person. Characters may all be performed by male or female actors. At the start of the scene, **Karen and Tony** *walk on talking to each other. The Bible-time actors are chatting off to one side.*

Karen: I don't know how we're ever going to finish our project on Paul.

Tony: Yeah. If we could just go back to Bible times and meet some of those Bible people. It would sure help.

Karen: Hey! Look over there. [*Pointing to the Bible-time friends*] They look like Bible-time people. Look how they're dressed.

Tony: Maybe they knew Paul. Let's ask them.

Karen: [*Walks over to friends*] Excuse me. Are you from Bible times?

BTF1: Why, yes we are.

Tony: Did you know the apostle Paul?

BTF2: [*Stops talking and turns attention to* **Karen and Tony**] Yes, we did.

Karen: We're on a research project about Paul and some of the things he taught.

BTF1: Well, perhaps we can help you. What is it specifically you need to know?

Tony: We're learning about cleaning out bad thoughts and actions.

BTF1: Oh, my. That's a good topic. Paul talked about that. In fact, he wrote a letter to our church about that very issue. But I'll let my friend start us off.

BTF2: One thing Paul taught us was that reading the Scriptures could help you to clean bad things out of your life.

BTF1: I agree. Reading the Scriptures helps you know what good things to keep and what bad things to get rid of. Paul was a good example of getting rid of the bad and keeping the good.

Karen: Could you tell us a little bit about what Paul was like?

BTF2: Yes. He was never jealous of what other people had. He was content (that means happy with) the things that he had. And he was a hard worker. He wasn't lazy.

BTF1: And don't forget that he often helped others.

BTF2: That's right. He certainly wasn't selfish with his time. He would pray for people when they got sick, help them out with a little extra money if they needed it, or just listen if someone had a problem they needed to talk about. He always said, "It's more blessed to give than to receive."

Karen: That's a good thing to remember.

BTF1: [*Looks up as if looking at the sun*] Oh, my. It's time for us to get a fire on for our lunch. It was good talking to you. [*Bible-time friends exit.*]

Tony: Wow! I wonder how they got here.

Karen: I don't know, but they sure helped us out a lot. Let's look in our Bible to see if Paul wrote anything in his letters about what to clean out of our lives.

Tony: Hey, here's something in his letter to the Ephesians—chapter 4, verses 31–32. He wrote, "Never shout angrily or say things to hurt others. Never do anything evil. Be kind and loving to each other. Forgive each other just as God forgave you in Christ." (ICB)

Karen: After all I've heard today, I think I'd better take some time out to look at the bad habits that are cluttering up my life.

Tony: No kidding. Me too. [*They exit.*]

COMPREHENSION QUESTIONS

Briefly discuss these questions with the children to clarify the main ideas in the Bible story presentation:

• **How does reading the Bible help us get rid of bad things?** (It helps us to know what the bad things are that we need to get rid of.)

• **How was Paul an example of getting rid of the bad things?** (He was content with what he had and not jealous of what others had; he worked hard and was not lazy; he gave to others rather than being selfish.)

• **What one thing did Paul always say?** (It is more blessed to give than to receive.)

• **What other things did Tony and Karen read about in Ephesians?** (Being kind and loving, forgiving others, not shouting angrily and saying mean things)

BIBLE BLUEPRINT MEMORY VERSE

Things You'll Need: Verse box with lid glued on two sides, a hammer and a chisel, a Bible, and a copy of this week's verse:

"Be a worker who is not ashamed of his work—a worker who uses the true teaching in the right way." 2 Timothy 2:15b (ICB)

You will need today's memory verse written on a large piece of paper. Fold it and put it in a Bible. Put the Bible in the verse box. The lid should be glued on two sides so that you will need a hammer and a chisel to get into it.

My verse box is fastened shut tighter and tighter every session now. You'd think someone was trying to challenge me with new ways to get it open. Well, today I'm going to have to use my hammer and chisel. Have another adult hold the box steady while you pry open one end. **Finally! Let's read our verse for today.** Pull out the Bible verse and read it with the group.

What does it mean when it says, "Be a worker who is not ashamed"? Allow kids to respond. Help them to see that cleaning out the bad thoughts and attitudes in our hearts and minds is one way we can be a worker who is not ashamed. **What does it mean when it says, "true teaching"?** Let the children respond. **That's right! The true teaching is God's Word. And we all want to be good workers who, with God's help, get rid of bad habits and attitudes. Now, to help you remember this verse, let's say it in a rhythm chant.** Teach kids the following:

Be a worker (clap-clap)
Be a worker (clap-clap)
Who is not ashamed of his work (clap-clap)
A worker (clap-clap)
Who uses (clap-clap)
The true teaching (clap-clap-clap)
In the right way. (clap-clap-clap)

Younger children may want to learn a shorter version of the Bible verse chant: "Be a worker who is not ashamed of his work."

Life Application
Small Group Time

Dismiss the children to their small group leaders, taking care to let the groups farthest away from the meeting area leave first. Each small group leader will need a copy of the Life Application Page for today. Be sure to give this page to leaders at least a week ahead of time so that they can be ready to work with their groups.

Children's Church Worship

Things You'll Need: *Bible Memory Toolbox* cassette, cassette player, and an offering container

If you are using this section, be sure to allow kids a short time to stand up and stretch in between activities. You might also want to include some active songs during the singing time.

SINGING

Choose music that correlates with this week's On-the-Job Training (Take out the trash) and the Action Step (Clean up garbage thoughts and actions). To reinforce this week's Bible Blueprint Verse, teach "Be a Worker" from page 121 of this book (also found on the *Bible Memory Toolbox* sing-along cassette tape).

CRITTER COUNTY STORY

Through the familiar and friendly Critter County characters, the children can see this week's theme in action and be motivated to clean up garbage thoughts and actions. This week's story begins on page 91.

OFFERING

Provide the children an opportunity to respond to God by giving. If you are using this curriculum for a children's church program, you may prefer to take the offering now instead of during Weekly Activities at the start of the Bible Story Time. Encourage children to thank God for something either verbally or silently as the offering plate passes by.

PRAISE AND PRAYER

Continue to help children through a prayer experience by saying one line of a prayer and asking them to repeat it. This week, ask children to think of one or two bad habits, thoughts, or actions they would like to clean up. (They don't need to share their ideas.) Conclude the prayer by asking God's help in taking out the trash.

Midweek Extras

Things You'll Need: 2 pieces of paper and a pencil for each student, trash cans (1 for every 8 to 10 children), a cassette player, and the *Bible Memory Toolbox* cassette

If you are using this curriculum for a midweek children's program or as a combined Sunday School/Children's Church program during the 50-Day Adventure, you may wish to add these fun activities to your time together.

GAME
Taking Out the Trash!

Begin by asking each child to write or draw symbols of two bad habits, thoughts, or actions, one on each of their strips of paper. Encourage them to include things they personally would like to clean up in their lives. Divide children into groups of eight to ten each, and circle them around a trash container. Take about five large steps backward.

(This can vary depending on the age of your students.) On the signal "go," have each student crumple and toss their papers of bad thoughts or actions into the trash can. Have them continue until all bad habits have been thrown away. Allow kids who want to, to tell what bad habits they are asking God to help them get rid of. Repeat the process as many times as you wish or have time for.

Adjustment for Younger Ages

The game leader will probably need to start the game by having a brainstorming time for kids to name examples of bad habits, thoughts, and actions. Then children may need suggestions for symbols they can draw to represent their bad habits, thoughts, or actions.

SINGING

Singing is a fun way to praise God. Make use of the songs included in this book, beginning on page 119. The songs in this book are also found on the *Bible Memory Toolbox* sing-along cassette tape. Be sure to learn the song, "Be a Worker," based on this week's Bible Blueprint Verse. And remember to include some active songs to give kids an opportunity to move around.

CRITTER COUNTY STORY

To Win Or Not to Win . . . What a Tough Question

It was election time again at the Critter County Elementary School. During this time, the students would elect some of their classmates to office. Someone would be chosen president, and someone else would get to be vice-president for the entire school year. It was an honor that most any critter would love to have. Especially Lunchbox!

Lunchbox is a delightful little lion cub filled with fun and mischief. He is never far from any trouble and seems to always be getting his tail caught in a place he shouldn't be. His dad, Lester, and his mom, Liona Lou, are always teaching him and telling him how he should live. Certainly someday he's going to get it.

Much to everyone's surprise, Lunchbox was nominated to run for vice-president, which means he got to make posters and speeches until the day that everyone would vote. He could tell the other critters what he would do to make their class and school a better place if he were elected.

It appeared to be a very close race between Lunchbox and Rascal the raccoon. It seemed like half the class was going to vote for Lunchbox and the other half had picked Rascal. Nobody could tell who was going to win. Lunchbox wanted to be vice-president so much that he made a very bad decision.

Every day for a week before the election, Lunchbox would go up to the other critters on the playground and ask how they were going to vote. If he was told that someone was going to vote for Rascal, he would offer that critter a dollar if he or she would change his or her mind and vote for Lunchbox instead. That was dishonest, because the critters were supposed to make up their own minds without getting any money. Lunchbox's plan backfired.

The day of the election finally came. All the critters went to vote, and at the end of the day, the votes were all counted. Rascal got almost ALL of the votes. Even the critters who had once planned to vote for Lunchbox had changed their minds. They didn't want a vice-president who would bribe critters for their votes.

That night, when Lunchbox was getting ready to go to bed in his lion's den, he told his dad what had happened. "Tell you one thing, Dad, I'm never again going to try and buy something that I can only be given."

"That's good, son," answered Lester. "Because when you tried to buy the votes, you sold a part of your good character—the honest part. And you need to keep ALL of that!"

Life Application Page

For Small Group Leaders

▶ **WEEK FIVE** ◀

ON-THE-JOB TRAINING TOPIC:

Take out the trash

ACTION STEP:

Clean up garbage thoughts and actions

BIBLE STORY:

Acts 20:32–38; Ephesians 4:26–32

MEMORY VERSE:

2 Timothy 2:15b (ICB)

THINGS YOU'LL NEED:

- Copy of "Tips for Small Group Leaders" from pages 23–24
- Action Step/Training Topic poster (made in advance)
- Children's Journal
- Adventure Prayer poster (made in advance)
- Children's Activity Book
- Newsprint
- Marker
- Chalkboard and chalk

IN ADVANCE:

Make a tool-shaped poster of the Adventure Prayer on page 24. Also make tool-shaped posters of the Action Step and On-the-Job Training Topic.

KID TALK

This week's On-the-Job Training Topic and Action Step focus on getting rid of bad habits, thoughts, and actions that clutter up our lives. It's important to stress that taking out the trash is an ongoing responsibility that God trusts each one of us with. It's our job to clean up our lives with his help.

Begin today's small group time by saying: **Let's take a look at our Training Topic and Action Step for today.** Point to posters. **Our topic is "Take out the trash." Our Action Step is "Clean up garbage thoughts and actions."** Have a brainstorming session to list all the bad habits, thoughts, and actions the kids can think of. Continue your discussion with the following questions:

• **How do you feel about people when they do or say something unkind?**

• **How do you feel about yourself when you realize you have done something that you shouldn't have?**

• **What are some things we heard about in our Bible story today that might be considered trash that needs to be taken out?**

• **Why is it important to take out the trash in our lives regularly?**

• **We've been talking a lot about taking out the trash and cleaning up our act today. What are the steps we have to take to get the job done?** You may wish to have the children come up with several easy steps that would include identification of bad habits, the action needed to clean them up or throw them away, and a follow-up procedure to ensure progress. Give the students an example of a bad habit that you have given up to pave the way toward using your time and talents more effectively. One example might be giving up watching too much television. That's hard to do if you really enjoy the shows that are on! But giving up television may also give you the time you need to read the Bible and help others more. What a great way to listen to God's Word, clean up your act, and use your tools well!

Ask students who have journals to answer this question: **Did you discover any new talents that you had this week?**

PRAYER TALK

Today during our prayer time, I want you to think about some of the garbage you'd like to clean out of your life. At the end of our prayer time together, ask for God's help in getting the job done. If you feel uncomfortable naming your bad habit, simply ask for God's help and guidance in getting rid of your garbage thoughts and actions.

Use the Adventure Prayer poster, reading together with your group. Close the prayer by allowing everyone in your group who feels comfortable to ask for God's help in taking out the trash. Allow time for special prayer concerns or requests any of the children may have.

Small Group Tip

Children can become easily embarrassed when talking about negative things in their lives. They often fear teasing, or being the only one who acts that way. Be sure to offer a great deal of reassurance during this session. Children who do admit to bad thoughts or actions will need confirmation that they are not alone. Remember to be thoughtful and kind. Never pressure a child into sharing something that he or she feels uncomfortable talking about. Just let children know that God is there for them whenever they need him, and they can talk to God silently or aloud!

▶ OVERVIEW ◀

On-the-Job Training Topic: Help in other places
Action Step: Take care of the world and its people
Bible Story: Acts 16:6–15
Memory Verse: Isaiah 58:10a (ICB)

GETTING STARTED

As the children arrive, they should stop by the Adventure check-in table to record their attendance, pick up their color-coded name tags, and meet their small group leaders. They can then proceed to work on the Bible-time project of their choice or move to the Bible Story Time with their small group leaders.

 ### Bible-Time Projects

Continue to offer ongoing projects, adding new ones as your schedule permits. Consider any new projects that correlate with this week's lesson.

 ### Bible Story Time

Gather the children together in a large group with their small group leaders.

WEEKLY ACTIVITIES

Welcome the children back to the Adventure. Proceed by making any necessary announcements, recognizing birthdays, or taking an offering. Remember not to spend too much time here so that your story presentation will not be rushed.

SETTING THE SCENE

Things You'll Need: Safety cones, construction worker clothes (an orange safety vest, work boots, hardhat [may be purchased at a party store], and jeans), hammer, nails, paint and brushes, a sawhorse, a piece of flat wood and the wooden Training Notice Post you used in Week 1, a cellular phone, a construction boot, and a copy of the Action Step

Preparation

Make the area look like a construction site. Dress in your construction crew work gear. Paint this week's On-the-Job Training Topic on a piece of wood, making it large enough for kids to read, and tuck a copy of this week's Action Step in the boot. Place the boot by the Training Notice Post.

Paint this week's Action Step on a piece of new lumber, ready to hang in your construction zone (stage area). You will also need a portable or cellular phone.

Topic Introduction

Hello! We've accomplished some terrific things since we've started our construction Adventure. Did all of you remember to take out the trash last week? I sure hope so. It can get pretty nasty when garbage piles up too long. It smells, too. Hold nose. **Who remembers what I'm talking about?** Allow children to respond. If you can arrange for someone to ring your phone at the start of the next part, that would be a terrific effect for the children! If not, simply pretend to hear a ringing sound. **Oh, boy, got a call on my portable phone. Sure is a good thing I brought it with me. A good construction crew worker is always listening to important directions so that good decisions can be made.** Answer phone. **Hello! What am I doing? I'm just talking with a terrific group of kids on the crew.** Cover the mouthpiece and say to the audience: **It's the boss. I think he wants to give us our next Training Topic.** Return to your phone call. **Yes, I'm listening. You're glad I'm helping in other places? Me too! I love helping in other places. I thought you were calling to give me this week's Training Topic.** Pause. **You are? Help in other places. Yes, sir, I am. Just tell me what this week's Training Topic is and I'll pass it right along.** Pause. **Oh, I heard you the first time. Help in other places. I will. As soon as I get off the phone, I'm going to share everything you have to say with the crew. Just tell me what to say.** Getting frustrated. **Help in other places? Listen, I promise that I will continue to help in other places the minute I hang up this phone. Now just pass along this week's Training Topic.** Really frustrated this time. **Look, I really mean it when I say that I'd love to help in other places. Why won't you believe me?** Pause. **You do believe me?** Pause. **Then why do you keep telling me to help in other places when you know that I will?** Longer pause here. Then look somewhat embarrassed. **Oh, I see. Help in other places IS this week's Training Topic. Well, I certainly won't forget it, you can count on that! Thanks a lot for calling. Oh, and I'm sorry about the mix-up. Talk to you soon. Bye!** Hang up the phone.

Who can tell me what this week's Training Topic is? Let children tell you. **You got it! "Help in other places." Now, let's see if our Action Step gives us an idea of how we can do that.** Invite a child up to pull the Action Step out of the work boot. **It says, "Take care of the world and its people." Both need to be treated carefully. If we take care of the people but forget the world, then there will be no place for the people to live. And if we take care of the world and not the people, then who will**

live in the beautiful world God gave us? Let's think about that as we watch the Bible story for today. Then we'll talk more later.

BIBLE STORY PRESENTATION

Bible Basis: *Acts 16:6–15*

Note: The Bible-time Drama Project on pages 30–32 provides ideas for a group of children to perform today's story. Ask the group to make their presentation at this time. If you chose not to offer this project, work together with your Bible Story Time leaders to prepare a drama, using the suggestions given in the project directions.

COMPREHENSION QUESTIONS

Briefly discuss these questions with the children to clarify the main ideas in the Bible story presentation:

• **What was Paul's vision?** (A man from Macedonia was begging him to come there and help them.)

• **What did Paul do after his vision?** (He knew that the vision was God's way of calling him to preach the gospel in Macedonia. Then he left to do just that.)

• **What happened when Paul spoke to the women gathered together on the Sabbath?** (A woman named Lydia opened her heart in response to Paul's message. She and the members of her household were then baptized, and she invited Paul and his friends to stay at her house.)

BIBLE BLUEPRINT MEMORY VERSE

Things You'll Need: Verse box with a combination lock on it, a cellular phone, a Bible, and a copy of this week's verse

"You should feed those who are hungry. You should take care of the needs of those who are troubled."
Isaiah 58:10a (ICB)

You will need today's memory verse written on a large piece of paper. Fold it and put it in a Bible, placing it inside the box used during previous sessions. Fasten your lid shut by using a coded combination padlock. You will also need the cellular phone from earlier in the session.

I've got a problem. Not only is my box shut, but it's locked. It's one of those combination locks that need a special code to get it open. But I don't know the code. What am I going to do? Hey, I'll just use my phone to call up the owner of the lock! Dial number, wait a moment, then proceed. **Hi, Brittany! Boy, am I glad I caught you at home. Remember that lock you let me borrow? Yeah, that's the one. Well, you didn't give me the special code I need to get it open again. 0-0-0** (insert whatever combination will open the lock). **Got it! Thanks for your help!**

OK, the combination is 0-0-0 (insert combination). Proceed to open the lock. Pull out the Bible and the verse. Let the children read the verse to you and repeat it one time. **This verse gave the people of Israel some suggestions for how they could take care of the world and its people. That's something we can do, too. Who are "the hungry" in modern times? Who are "the troubled"?** Allow children to respond. **What can we do to help these people?** (Adopt an orphan child with our family; give money, clothes, and food to a homeless shelter; give Christmas presents to the children of those in prison, and so on.) Have the group repeat the verse with you one more time.

Younger children may want to learn a shorter version of the Bible verse with these actions:

You should take care (Point out then hug self.)
Of the needs (Hold out both hands as if waiting for something.)
Of those who are troubled. (Put index fingers beside each side of mouth and make a sad face.)

Life Application
Small Group Time

Dismiss the children to their small group leaders, taking care to let the groups farthest away from the meeting area leave first. Each small group leader will need a copy of the Life Application Page for today. Be sure to give this page to leaders at least a week ahead of time so that they can be ready to work with their groups.

Children's Church Worship

Things You'll Need: *Bible Memory Toolbox* cassette, a cassette player, and an offering container

If you are using this section, be sure to allow kids a short time to stand up and stretch in between activities. You might also want to include some active songs during the singing time.

SINGING

Choose music that correlates with this week's On-the-Job Training Topic (Help in other places) and the Action Step (Take care of the world and its people). To reinforce this week's Bible Blueprint Verse, teach "Take Care of Their Needs," from page 121 of this book (also found on the *Bible Memory Toolbox* sing-along cassette tape).

CRITTER COUNTY STORY

Through the familiar and friendly Critter County characters, the children can see this week's theme in action and be motivated to help in other places and spread God's Word to others. This week's story begins on page 99.

OFFERING

Provide the children an opportunity to respond to God by giving. If you are using this curriculum for a children's church program, you may prefer to take the offering now instead of during Weekly Activities at the start of the Bible Story Time. Encourage children to thank God for something either verbally or silently as the offering plate passes by.

PRAISE AND PRAYER

Continue to help children through a prayer experience by saying one line of a prayer and asking them to repeat it. This week, challenge children to think of ways to reach out to people in need, especially people they may not know. At the close of your prayer, invite children to share their ideas with God.

 Midweek Extras

Things You'll Need: 2" x 2" square pieces of paper, pencils, straws, a cassette player, and the *Bible Memory Toolbox* cassette

If you are using this curriculum for a midweek children's program or as a combined Sunday School/Children's Church program during the Construction Crew Adventure, you may wish to add these fun activities to your time together.

GAME

Pass It On!

Create teams of eight to ten children each. Have them sit beside each other. Then, give each child a 2" x 2" square piece of paper, a pencil, and a straw. Tell each person to write down one way to take care of the world and its people. After kids are done, start the game by having the teams race to pass on their ideas to teammates using a straw (hands cannot be used to hold the papers after the writing is completed).

To play, each child should put the straw in his or her mouth and bend over to pick up the idea paper by sucking air in through the straw. Children then will pass on their idea to the neighbor who is waiting to receive it with his or her straw, and so on down the line. (If the paper drops, children must pick it up by using their straw!) The person at the end of the line must rush around to join the person at the beginning of the line until everyone has their own idea back again. At the end of the game, let everyone read his or her idea aloud.

Adjustment for Younger Ages

Have children draw pictures of ways they can take care of the world and its people. Then, rather than using straws, have children pass their idea papers in an over-the-head relay. At the end of the game, all children should have their own papers back. Make sure they each have only one paper at a time in their hands during the game.

SINGING

Singing is a fun way to praise God. Make use of the songs included in this book, beginning on page 119. The songs in this book are also found on the *Bible Memory Toolbox* sing-along cassette tape. Be sure to learn the song "Take Care of Their Needs," based on this week's Bible Blueprint Verse. And remember to include some active songs to give kids an opportunity to move around.

CRITTER COUNTY STORY

A Day She'll NEVER Forget

It was the worst of all mouse nightmares. Nothing can be harder on a little mouse than a tail injury! Because their tails are so long, if they hurt, they REALLY hurt. And if they are even the least little bit sore, it's so hard to walk, because they have to drag their tail over the floor. Can you just imagine how it must hurt?

So when Millicent the mouse got her tail hurt by someone setting a trash can on it, it was awful. But the worst of it was she had no home and no friends. Millicent was new in Critter County, and she hadn't found a job yet. She also had a hard time finding food to eat. For sleeping, she had made a little nest outside the Critter County Church. But, with the weather getting colder and now with a hurt tail, she was very discouraged.

Millicent slowly made her way to her nest. Oh, how her tail hurt. When she got there she very gently laid her tail on the ground and lay down to sleep.

Now, inside the church, Liona Lou the lion was having a tea for a critter friend of hers who was getting married. All of the critters were having a great time. Little did they know that a poor, hungry, and sick little mouse was sleeping right outside the door.

After the tea, Liona Lou was cleaning up. She had wiped down the tables and washed all the dishes. *After I get this trash out,* she thought, *then I'll be able to go home and take a nap.* She grabbed her coat and hat. Then she grabbed the trash bag and scurried out to deposit it in the trash bin. As she was heading back into the church, she stopped. *What is that?* she thought. *It sounds like someone is hurt.* Liona Lou followed the soft whimper along the side of the church building until she saw Millicent's nest.

"What have we here?" she asked looking in on Millicent. At first Millicent was terrified. Lions are cats, and cats don't treat mice kindly. But Millicent noticed that Liona Lou had a kind look in her eyes.

"Oh, my name is Millicent," answered the tiny mouse. "Millicent from Milwaukee."

"Well, Millicent, what are you doing out here? And why are you crying?" asked Liona Lou.

Millicent answered, "I lost my job in Milwaukee and came to Critter County hoping to find a job. I don't have one yet, and because of that I don't have a home. And someone set a trash can on my tail, and it's hurting so bad. I don't know anyone and I don't know what to do!" Millicent started to cry harder.

"There, there," said Liona Lou soothingly. "You've got a friend now. I'll help you. You just lie quietly and I'll go get Dr. Duck." When Dr. Duck came he took a look at Millicent's tail. Fortunately, it wasn't too serious.

Dr. Duck said, "But she'll need a place to stay until her tail gets better and she can find some work."

"She can stay with us as long as she wants to," answered Liona Lou. "We'll take good care of her. And maybe my Lester can help her get a job at his gas station. He's always looking for good workers. Thank you, Dr. Duck."

"Thank you, Liona Lou," whispered Millicent. "You have been very kind to me, even though you don't know me. I will never forget your kindness."

Notes

Life Application Page

For Small Group Leaders

▶ WEEK SIX ◀

ON-THE-JOB TRAINING TOPIC:
Help in other places

ACTION STEP:
Take care of the world and its people

BIBLE STORY:
Acts 16:6–15

MEMORY VERSE:
Isaiah 58:10a (ICB)

THINGS YOU'LL NEED:

- Copy of "Tips for Small Group Leaders" on pages 23–24
- Action Step/Training Topic poster (made in advance)
- Children's Journal
- Adventure Prayer poster (made in advance)
- Children's Activity Book
- Newsprint
- Marker
- Chalkboard and chalk

IN ADVANCE:

Make a tool-shaped poster of the Adventure Prayer on page 24. Also make tool-shaped posters of the Action Step and On-the-Job Training Topic.

KID TALK

Show this week's Action Step and Training Topic. If you have chosen to involve your group in a missions project, explain it to them at this time. If not, begin your session by having the group brainstorm ways they can help others in foreign countries as well as the needy nearby. If you wish to emphasize taking care of the world, encourage kids to brainstorm ways they can recycle the items they use each day. List their ideas on newsprint or a chalkboard. Continue your discussion by using these questions:

• **The Bible verse for today says, "You should feed those who are hungry. You should take care of the needs of those who are troubled" Isaiah 58:10a (ICB). What is something you can do at home for people in need?**

• **What are some projects you are aware of that are helping people in your community?**

• **Are any of you involved in any missions projects?** (Like supporting a child in another country, serving dinner at a homeless shelter, delivering food baskets at holiday times, and so on) **Tell us about them.**

• **We've talked a bit about how to help take care of people in foreign places, but how can we take care of the world, too?** This question is designed to help kids to think about recycling

Don't forget to review previous Action Steps and Training Topics. Ask the children in your group to share something they enjoyed doing in their journals this week.

PRAYER TALK

Start by asking: **Can you think of someone who is hungry or troubled? Let's read our Adventure Prayer together and at the end, pray for the person you are thinking of.** Also ask children if they have any special prayer concerns, and be sure to make time for them, too.

Small Group Tip

When talking to your group about prayer, help children to understand that God will listen to anything they have to say. Assure students that they don't have to create perfect sentences with specific words for God to listen to them. Some students may still be uncomfortable praying aloud in their own words. Tell these students to share their thoughts with God silently, and confirm that God will hear everything they have to say.

▶ OVERVIEW ◀

On-the-Job Training Topic: Meet with the Master Builder

Action Step: Meet God through prayer and praise

Bible Story: Acts 4:23–31

Memory Verse: Psalm 92:1 (ICB)

GETTING STARTED

As the children arrive, they should stop by the Adventure check-in table to record their attendance, pick up their color-coded name tags, and meet their small group leaders. They can then proceed to work on the Bible-Time Project of their choice or move to the Bible Story Time with their small group leaders.

 ## Bible-Time Projects

Continue to offer ongoing projects, adding new ones as your schedule permits. Consider any new projects that correlate with this week's lesson.

 ## Bible Story Time

Gather the children together in a large group with their small group leaders.

WEEKLY ACTIVITIES

Welcome the children back to the Adventure. Proceed by making any necessary announcements, recognizing birthdays, or taking an offering. Remember not to spend too much time here so that your story presentation will not be rushed.

SETTING THE SCENE

Things You'll Need: Safety cones, construction worker clothes (an orange safety vest, work boots, hardhat [may be purchased at a party store], and jeans), hammer, nails, paint and brushes, a sawhorse, a piece of flat wood and the wooden Training Notice Post you used in Week 1, a construction boot, and a copy of the Action Step (written in a rebus style)

Preparation

Make the area look like a construction site. Dress in your construction crew work gear. Paint this week's On-the-Job Training Topic on a piece of wood, making it large enough for kids to read, and tuck a copy of this week's Action Step (written as a rebus) in the boot. Place the boot by the Training Notice Post.

  God through

 and

103

Topic Introduction

Hello! This week's On-the-Job Training Topic is "Meet with the Master Builder!" First, does anyone know who the Master Builder is? Allow children to respond. **Right! The Master Builder is God. How do you think we can meet with the Master Builder? Can we call him on the phone? E-mail him on our computer?** Encourage response and discussion. **Now, let's take a look at our Action Step for this week to see if it will help.** Have a child come up and pull the rebus out of the boot. Show it to the group. **Oh, my! It seems to be written in a puzzle. Can anyone figure out what it means?** Allow kids to talk about what they think it means. Then say it together with the group. **"Meet God through prayer and praise." When do people tend to pray more, when life is easy or when life is hard?** Allow time for kids to answer. **When is it easiest to praise God? When is it hardest?** Allow time for kids to answer. **Today's Bible story is about people who learned how to get through some hard times by meeting with God. Then we'll hear a story about a modern-day person who is learning this same lesson.**

BIBLE STORY PRESENTATION

Bible Basis: Acts 4:23–31
Characters: A Leader to read the
                      Bible story and one to
                      tell Dave's story

Things You'll Need
(optional):   Television
                      Video cassette player

A copy of Dave Dravecky's book, Comeback, *with Tim Stafford, published by Zondervan, © 1990 (to show pictures to kids), or Dave's story on video cassette (available by calling 1-800-727-8004)*

Before reading the Bible passage for today, explain to the kids that Peter and John have just been released from jail. They had been put there overnight because of telling others about Jesus and praying for a man to be healed. The believers were frightened that they too would be put in prison for telling others about Jesus. Ask, **What did they do? Let's read the Bible passage to find out.** Read Acts 4:23-31 out of a children's Bible if possible. Then ask the kids, **What did the believers do when they were afraid?** (Answers could include: They prayed; they asked God for help; they praised God.) **These are things God wants us to do, too—not just when we're afraid, but all the time. Now, I want to tell you a true story about a modern-day person who, like the believers, has gone through some pretty scary things. But he is learning to meet with the Master Builder to help him each day. His name is Dave Dravecky.** If you rented the suggested video you will want to show it now. If not, tell this shortened version of his story showing pictures from the book, *Comeback,* if you have that.

When Dave Dravecky was a little boy, he loved to play baseball. He and his dad would often play catch in the backyard until dark. As Dave grew up his love of baseball continued. He played baseball in junior high, high school, and college. He was a very good left-handed pitcher. And more than anything else, he wanted to play professional baseball. As a young man, he was picked to play on a couple of minor league practice teams. Over time if you're good enough, you get picked to play on a major league team. While playing on one of these practice teams, Dave

and his wife Jan became Christians.

Dave continued to practice, and one day it happened. He got called up to be the pitcher for a major league team, the San Diego Padres. He played for them a while and then went to play for the San Francisco Giants. Then, one day, he noticed a small lump on his pitching arm. *It's probably nothing*, he thought. But after a while he thought he'd better get it checked by a doctor. As he and his wife waited for the report to come, they prayed that God would be with them whether the report was bad or good. It wasn't good. Dave had cancer.

Dave had surgery to take the cancer out of his pitching arm, and he was told that he would probably never pitch again. This was in October of 1988. He and his wife were scared and upset. But they continued to pray. And others prayed for them. Praying helped them to remember that God loved them and was with them. And it helped them to have courage.

After his arm had started to heal, Dave started practicing his pitching again. The doctor said as long as he was careful, he could at least practice. He practiced and practiced. And believe it or not, he *did* pitch again. On August 10, 1989, he pitched for his team, the San Francisco Giants. It was a miracle! Even the doctor couldn't believe it. But then five days later, on August 15, Dave's arm broke while he was pitching another game. Again he, his wife, and his family and friends prayed.

Dave had more surgeries, but his arm was getting worse instead of better. In 1991 he realized that he would not be able to pitch again. Once more, Dave and his wife prayed that God would help them. Dave and his family went through some very hard times. There were days when they felt angry, scared, and alone. But they continued to pray, because they knew God would help them through. And he did.

Today, Dave and his wife help other people who are scared or upset. They tell these people about Jesus and how he can help them, too. They write letters to people and speak all over the country. And

Dave has taken up a new sport—golfing! Even though Dave's life has been hard, he is learning that meeting with the Master Builder each day through prayer and praise will help him and his family to get through the tough times.

COMPREHENSION QUESTIONS

Briefly discuss these questions with the children to clarify the main ideas in the Bible story presentation:

• **Why were the believers scared?** (Peter and John had been put in jail and told not to talk about Jesus anymore.)

• **What did the believers do when they were scared?** (They prayed.)

• **What was Dave Dravecky's job?** (He was a pitcher for the Giants.)

• **Why did he have to stop pitching?** (He got cancer.)

• **What did Dave do when he got scared?** (He prayed.)

• **How did praying help him and his family?** (It gave them hope. It helped them to remember that God loved them and was with them. It gave them courage to face whatever happened.)

BIBLE BLUEPRINT MEMORY VERSE

Things You'll Need: Verse box with the lid locked on with a keyed lock, the lock key and several other keys, a Bible, a copy of the verse, and chalk and a chalkboard or a chart and markers

"It is good to praise the Lord, to sing praises to God Most High." Psalm 92:1 (ICB)

You will need today's memory verse written on a large piece of paper. Fold it and put it in a Bible, placing it inside the box used during previous sessions. Close your lid and lock it.

Well, here is our trusty verse box. But once again, we have to figure out how to get into the box. What do we need? (A key.) **I have a number of keys here with me today. Let's hope one of them works.**

Invite kids to try different keys. **Well, I only have one more left. Let's try it.** Use the lock key. Take out the verse for today. Read it to the group, and then ask them to repeat it with you. **"It is good to praise the Lord, to sing praises to God Most High" Psalm 92:1 (ICB). That was great! How can we praise him?** (In prayer, song, worship dance, celebration, by the things we do and so on.) **Why do we praise him?** (It is our way of showing appreciation, love, and respect for him and all he has done! It's our way of paying God compliments.) **Now, let's see how many things we can name in one minute that we can praise God for.** When you say, "Go!" let kids shout out reasons to praise God as you list them on a chalkboard or chart. **Wow! Look at all those things we listed to praise God for! Let's remember some of these this week.**

Younger children may want to learn a shorter version of the Bible verse: "It is good to praise the Lord" Psalm 92:1a (ICB). This is a good opportunity to let younger children know that we praise God during worship with one another. Sing a praise song, asking children to clap their hands or dance with you as you sing. Let them enjoy the chance to praise the Lord!

Life Application

Small Group Time

Dismiss the children to their small group leaders, taking care to let the groups farthest away from the meeting area leave first. Each small group leader will need a copy of the Life Application Page for today. Be sure to give this page to leaders at least a week ahead of time so that they can be ready to work with their groups.

Children's Church Worship

Things You'll Need: *Bible Memory Toolbox* cassette, a cassette player, and an offering container

If you are using this section, be sure to allow kids a short time to stand up and stretch in between activities. You might also want to include some active songs during the singing time.

SINGING

Choose music that correlates with this week's Construction Crew On-the-Job Training (Meet with the Master Builder) and the Action Step (Experience God's love). To reinforce this week's Bible Blueprint Memory Verse, teach "It Is Good to Praise the Lord," from page 122 of this book (also found on the *Bible Memory Toolbox* sing-along cassette tape.)

CRITTER COUNTY STORY

Through the familiar and friendly Critter County characters, the children can see this week's theme in action and be motivated to experience God's love. This week's story begins on page 108.

OFFERING

Provide the children an opportunity to respond to God by giving. If you are using this curriculum for a children's church program, you may prefer to take the offering now instead of during Weekly Activities at the start of the Bible Story Time. Encourage children to thank God for something either verbally or silently as the offering plate passes by.

PRAISE AND PRAYER

Continue to help children through a prayer experience by saying one line of a prayer and asking them to repeat it. This week, ask the group to recall the reasons to praise God they named during the memory verse time. Conclude your prayer by letting the group shout out their reasons in praise to the Lord!

Things You'll Need: A small wooden cube (or paper cube, pattern on page 125) and marker for each child, chalkboard and chalk or newsprint and markers, a cassette player, and the *Bible Memory Toolbox* cassette

If you are using this curriculum for a midweek children's program or as a combined Sunday School/Children's Church program during the Adventure, you can add these fun activities to your time together.

GAME

Building Blocks with God

If you have a large group, divide the children into smaller groups of four to seven. Ask the groups to use their markers to put the following words or symbols on each of the six sides of their cubes. (If you are using the paper cube pattern from p. 125, let the children draw their designs *before* taping the cubes together.)

1) Y O U
2) Smiling face
3) A teardrop
4) A cross
5) A book
6) J E S U S

Display the following cube directions on a chalkboard or newsprint for all to see during the game:

1) Y O U -   A time you can pray
2) Smiling face - Something you can praise God for
3) A teardrop -   Someone you know who needs prayer
4) A cross -   Something you may need to ask forgiveness for
5) A book -   Your favorite Bible story
6) J E S U S -   Something you appreciate about Jesus

In each small group, kids take turns rolling the cubes. Ask children to respond by sharing a brief story that correlates to the cube directions that match the word or symbol that landed face up after the roll. Tell kids they need only share stories they are comfortable explaining to others.

Adjustment for Younger Ages

The game leader may need to make decorated cubes ahead of time. Explain to children what each side of the cube represents. Then the leader will need to stay with the group to remind them what they need to do each time the cube is rolled.

SINGING

Singing is a fun way to praise God. Make use of the songs included in this book, beginning on page 119. The songs in this book are also found on the *Bible Memory Toolbox* sing-along cassette tape. Be sure to learn the song "It Is Good to Praise the Lord," based on this week's Bible Blueprint Verse. And remember to include some active songs to give kids an opportunity to move around.

CRITTER COUNTY STORY

Where's Noah When You Need Him?

It seemed like the great flood all over again. All the critters in the county were asking the same question: "Is it EVER going to stop raining?" And it was no wonder they were asking, because it had been raining and raining and then it rained some more. In fact, Elle the elephant couldn't remember when it HADN'T been raining.

And not only had the critters' spirits grown wet and soggy, so had the ground! The corn fields looked like lakes, and small creeks had become rushing rivers. Dr. Duck was treating critter after critter in his office. Many were suffering from colds and sore throats. Poor Gertrude the giraffe had a TERRIBLE sore throat. And when she gets a sore throat, it takes the medicine a lo-o-o-ong time to get to the bottom of the pain.

The forecast didn't look much better. Waldo the weather weasel could only predict a 90% chance of rain for the next six days. Finally, when the roof was blown off Sydney the squirrel's tree house, everyone decided to meet at the Critter County Church for a special meeting.

Most of the critters had to dress to keep really dry just so they'd arrive at the church safely. Liona Lou the lion wore a flashy, bright red fireman's coat and hat that had belonged to her Uncle Leonard. Her husband Lester was warm and dry in his ski clothes. Since there had developed such a shortage of umbrellas, some of the raccoons kept bunnies and kittens dry by carrying them.

The ducks paddled their way onto the driveway and waddled into the church. Although they and the turtles actually liked all the rain, they were all upset because it was causing such a hardship on their friends.

The service started. Pastor Penguin began by suggesting the group sing several songs together. The singing started off rather slowly, but by the time the critters had sung four or five songs, their voices were lifting so high and loud, they forgot all their problems outside. In fact, the longer they sang praises to Jesus, the more their troubles and sadness floated away. Songs of joy . . . songs of praise. The music filled the whole valley. Before anyone realized it, two and a half hours had gone by. And when Liona Lou excused herself to freshen up, she couldn't believe her eyes as she passed by the front door.

"Oh, my!" she screamed. Lester thought she had fallen so he rushed to her side. Several otters and ostriches joined him, and none could believe what they saw as they pressed their beaks against the door. The rain had stopped and the sun was shining.

Life Application Page

For Small Group Leaders

▶ WEEK SEVEN ◀

ON-THE-JOB TRAINING TOPIC:

Meet with the Master Builder

ACTION STEP:

Meet God through prayer and praise

BIBLE STORY:

Acts 4:23–31

MEMORY VERSE:

Psalm 92:1 (ICB)

THINGS YOU'LL NEED:

- Copy of "Tips for Small Group Leaders" from pages 23–24
- Action Step/Training Topic poster (made in advance)
- Children's Journal
- Adventure Prayer poster (made in advance)
- Children's Activity Book
- Newsprint
- Marker
- Chalkboard and chalk

IN ADVANCE:

Make a tool-shaped poster of the Adventure Prayer on page 24. Also make tool-shaped posters of the Action Step and On-the-Job Training Topic.

KID TALK

Show Action Step and Training posters for this week. **This week's On-the-Job-Training Topic is "Meet with the Master Builder." One way we do that is by practicing this week's Action Step, which is, "Meet God through prayer and praise." Let's talk about these as we think about today's stories.** Use some of the following questions:

- **In our stories today, who was scared?** (The believers and Dave Dravecky.)
- **What types of things make you scared?**
- **What can you do when you get scared?** (Talk to an adult, pray, think about a Bible verse, and so on.)
- **How do you feel, knowing that God is with you every day wherever you go?** Be prepared for some children to respond with worry or fear. Follow up those responses by telling children that God's presence is always welcome because he is a loving and forgiving God, no matter what we do.

- **What are some specific ways we can meet with the Master Builder?** (Through worship, prayer, song, learning, responding to God's Word in what we say and do.)

Did any of you learn something new from your journal last week about taking care of the world and its people? Allow time for kids to respond.

Each week we've been learning how to build a church where everyone can feel welcomed and loved! Let's celebrate that together now in prayer.

PRAYER TALK

Today we'll finish our Adventure Prayer by praising God. Think of one or two things you would like to say in praise to God. They can be thanksgivings, celebrations, observations, or whatever you choose.

Using your Adventure Prayer poster, read it together with your group. Finish by asking each person in your group who wishes to, to share his or her praises with God. Ask group members if they have any special prayer concerns or requests, and be sure to include them, also.

Small Group Tip

Some children, especially younger ones, will have trouble understanding what it means to "Meet with the Master Builder." Children may focus on ideas that relate to heaven, what happens after death, and meeting God then. Let them share thoughts about this, but emphasize the experiential opportunities we have as we live our lives here on earth! To help them do this, ask young people what it means to be a disciple. (To read and listen to Bible stories, to pray, to treat people the way Jesus would, to obey what God tells us to do in the Bible, and so on.) Then stretch their thinking to include ways that God can be a part of that process!

WEEK eight

▶ **OVERVIEW** ◀

On-the-Job Training Topic: Celebrate the best club ever
Action Step: Give thanks that Jesus is alive
Bible Story: Acts 9:1–19
Memory Verse: 1 Peter 2:9 (NIV)

GETTING STARTED

As the children arrive, they should stop by the Adventure check-in table to record their attendance, pick up their color-coded name tags, and meet their small group leaders. They can then proceed to work on the Bible-time project of their choice or move to the Bible Story Time with their small group leaders.

 Bible-Time Projects

Continue to offer ongoing projects, adding new ones as your schedule permits. Consider any new projects that correlate with this week's lesson.You'll need to complete all your projects during this last session.

 Bible Story Time

Gather the children together in a large group with their small group leaders.

WEEKLY ACTIVITIES

Welcome the children back to the Adventure. Proceed by making any necessary announcements, recognizing birthdays, or taking an offering. Remember not to spend too much time here so that your story presentation will not be rushed.

SETTING THE SCENE

Things You'll Need: Safety cones, construction worker clothes (an orange safety vest, work boots, hardhat [may be purchased at a party store], and jeans), hammer, nails, paint and brushes, a sawhorse, a piece of flat wood and the wooden Training Notice Post you used in Week 1 with all topics attached, a helium-filled balloon, Action Steps from previous weeks, a construction boot, and a copy of this week's Action Step

Preparation

Make the area look like a construction site. Dress in your construction crew work gear. Paint this week's On-the-Job Training Topic on a piece of wood. Make it large enough for kids to read. Tuck a copy of this week's Action Step in the boot. Place the boot by the Training Notice Post. Tie the balloon to your wrist.

If you offered the Bible-time worship dance project, the children may have prepared a celebratory dance for your gathering today. Use it to prepare the kids for the Bible story. You may also wish to decorate your construction zone in a celebratory manner.

Topic Introduction

Hello! Can you believe this is the last week of our Adventure? Wave arms around a lot as you talk so the balloon becomes a nuisance to you. **I need your help to review a little bit today. Let's look at our On-the-Job**

Training Topics and Action Steps for the past several weeks.

This balloon is really getting in my way. I know I put it on my wrist to remind me of something, but I can't remember what! Oh, well, maybe I'll think of it as we review. Tell me what each of these mean. Allow kids to help you review the Training Topics and Action Steps as you point to the topics and hold up Action Step papers.

We've learned so much about building a church where everyone can feel welcomed and loved! I feel like celebrating! Celebrating! That's it! I put the balloon on my wrist to remind me of today's Training Topic. Post the topic. "Celebrate the best club ever!" Who can tell me why the church (or church club) is the best club ever? Allow kids to respond. Answers might include, anyone can belong, Jesus is the Head of the club, it will last forever and ever, everyone can feel loved, it's all over the world, and so on. What are some of the ways we can celebrate our church or church club? I think we'll get a hint from this week's Action Step. Invite a child to pull the Action Step out of the work boot. Read it. "Give thanks that Jesus is alive." That's a great way to celebrate the best club ever. Are there any other ways? Allow kids to make suggestions. These might include doing a celebratory dance, having a party, inviting others to come see what church (or church club) is all about, singing, and so on. If you have a group that prepared the celebratory dance during project time, have them come and share it with the group now. That was great! Now, we have a special Bible story. Let's see what it is!

BIBLE STORY PRESENTATION

Bible Basis:	Acts 9:1–19
Characters:	Narrator
	Saul (Mime 1),
	Ananias (Mime 2)
Things You'll Need:	Black–and–white mime face makeup (may be purchased at a costume or theatrical shop)

Today's Bible story is read by a narrator while two mimes pantomime the actions accordingly. Your mimes actors can be clowns, persons dressed in black with a white face, or they can do this without any makeup or costume at all. Put your own creativity into the presentation! The actions in brackets should be performed as the Narrator speaks so that there is no hesitation in the flow of the story.

Narrator: There was a man named Saul who was very angry and mean to God's people. [*Saul makes a fist and looks angrily toward the audience.*] After receiving authority to arrest Christians, he journeyed to a place called Damascus. [*Saul receives orders and looks toward a faraway land.*] As he neared Damascus, a light from heaven flashed all around him. [*Saul looks shocked and terrified.*] Saul fell to the ground in fear, and he heard a voice say to him, "Saul, Saul, why do you persecute me?" [*Saul falls to the ground, and carefully glances up as Jesus speaks.*]

"Who are you, Lord?" Saul asked. [*Saul turns heavenward while on his knees, and spreads his hands in wonder.*] "I am Jesus, whom you are persecuting," he replied. "Now get up and go into the city, and you will be told what you must do." But as Saul got up from the ground and opened his eyes, he couldn't see. So the men traveling with him led Saul into Damascus. [*Saul gets up, opens his eyes, and acts blind. He is led off stage.*]

In Damascus there was a disciple named Ananias. The Lord also called to him in a vision, "Ananias!" [*Ananias enters and falls to his knees as the Lord calls his name.*] "Yes, Lord," he answered.

The Lord told him, "Go to the house of Judas on Straight Street and ask for a man named Saul. He will be praying. In a vision he has seen you come and place your hands on him to restore his sight."

"Lord," Ananias answered, "I have heard that this man has harmed many believers. And he has come here to arrest all who call on your name." [*Ananias looks to the heavens and shakes his head no.*]

But the Lord told Ananias, "Go! This man is my chosen leader who will suffer, but do great things in my name. [*Ananias gets up, nods his head yes, and exits. Then Saul enters and proceeds center stage to pray.*]

Ananias found Saul and placed his hands on him. [*Ananias enters the stage and walks toward Saul.*] He said, "Jesus has sent me so that you may see again and be filled with the Holy Spirit." [*Ananias places his hands on Saul's eyes.*]

Immediately, Saul could see again. [*Saul opens his eyes and reaches out toward Ananias in friendship.*] Saul got up and was baptized. How glad he was to be a part of God's family and that Jesus was, is, and always will be alive! His new job would be to tell anyone who would listen about the best club ever, God's church, and its leader, Jesus. [*Saul turns to shake Ananias' hand.*]

At this point **Saul and Ananias** could distribute a gift for children to take home with them. It could be a small cross to represent that Jesus is alive, or something else of your own choosing.

COMPREHENSION QUESTIONS

Briefly discuss these questions with the children to clarify the main ideas in the Bible story presentation:

• **What happened to Saul as he traveled to Damascus to put the followers of Jesus in prison?** (A light flashed and Jesus spoke to him. He told Saul to get up and go into the city, where he would be told what to do.)

• **What happened to Saul when he got up? What did he do?** (When Saul got up,

he was blind. He let himself be led to Damascus where he prayed and waited for Ananias to come.)

• **What did Ananias do for Saul?** (He followed God's orders to go to Saul and place his hands on him so that he could see again. Then he baptized Saul.)

• **What was Saul's new job?** (To tell anyone who would listen about the best club ever, God's church, and its leader, Jesus.)

BIBLE BLUEPRINT MEMORY VERSE

Things You'll Need: Verse box with lid, a Bible, and a copy of the verse

"You are a chosen people, . . . a people belonging to God, that you may declare the praises of him who called you out of darkness into his wonderful light."
1 Peter 2:9 (NIV)

You will need today's memory verse written on a large piece of paper. Fold it and put it in a Bible, placing it inside the box used during previous sessions.

During our final celebration of the best club ever, we want to look at one more Bible Blueprint Verse. And today, all we need to do is to lift the top off. Invite a child to take out the verse for today. Read it to the group, and then ask them to repeat it with you. **"You are a chosen people, . . . a people belonging to God, that you may declare the praises of him who called you out of darkness into his wonderful light"** 1 Peter 2:9. **This verse refers to people who believe in Jesus when it says "You are a chosen people."** Allow kids to respond to these questions: **Who does the choosing? What are the believers chosen to do? What does it mean when it says that God called the Bible-time Christians out of darkness into his wonderful light?** (He helped them to understand the truth about who Jesus is and to accept him as God's Son and their Savior from sin.) **Does God still call people "out of darkness into his wonderful light" today?** To help kids practice the verse, divide them into six groups. Have each group be responsible for saying one part of the verse as follows:

Group 1: You are a chosen people, . . .
Group 2: A people belonging to God,
Group 3: That you may declare
Group 4: The praises of him
Group 5: Who called you out of darkness
Group 6: Into his wonderful light.

Younger children may want to learn a shorter version of the Bible verse: "You are a chosen people, . . . a people belonging to God" 1 Peter 2:9a (NIV).

Life Application
Small Group Time

Dismiss the children to their small group leaders, taking care to let the groups farthest away from the meeting area leave first. Each small group leader will need a copy of the Life Application Page for today. Be sure to give this page to leaders at least a week ahead of time so that they can be ready to work with their groups.

Children's Church Worship

Things You'll Need: *Bible Memory Toolbox* cassette, a cassette player, and an offering container

If you are using this section, be sure to allow kids a short time to stand up and stretch in between activities. You might also want to include some active songs during the singing time.

SINGING

Choose music that correlates with this week's On-the-Job Training Topic (Celebrate the best club ever) and the Action Step (Give thanks that Jesus is alive). To reinforce this week's Bible Blueprint Verse, teach "You Are a Chosen People," from page 122 of this book (also found on the *Bible Memory Toolbox* sing-along cassette tape).

CRITTER COUNTY STORY

Through the familiar and friendly Critter County characters, the children can see this week's theme in action and be motivated to respond as a child of God while celebrating the best club ever. This week's story begins on page 115.

OFFERING

Provide the children an opportunity to respond to God by giving. If you are using this curriculum for a children's church program, you may prefer to take the offering now instead of during Weekly Activities at the start of the Bible Story Time. Encourage children to thank God for something either verbally or silently as the offering plate passes by.

PRAISE AND PRAYER

Continue to help children through a prayer experience by saying one line of a prayer and asking them to repeat it. This week, ask the group to think of a reason to celebrate the church or their church club as the best club ever. Conclude your prayer by letting the group share their celebrations to the Lord!

Midweek Extras

Things You'll Need: Paper bag for each team, written instructions and materials for each team as directed in the game section, a cassette player, and the *Bible Memory Toolbox* cassette

If you are using this curriculum for a midweek children's program or as a combined Sunday School/Children's Church program during the 50-Day Adventure, you may wish to add these fun activities to your time together.

GAME

Celebrate the Best Club Ever

Divide the group into two teams. Provide each team with a paper bag that contains written instructions for each member of the team, as well as any materials needed to complete the instruction. Each instruction will be related to kids celebrating the best club ever or rejoicing that Jesus is alive. (Instruction ideas are listed below.)

To play the game, put the bags filled with instructions and materials on the opposite side of the room from the teams. On "go," tell the first person on each team to run to the bag, pull out one instruction, and complete it. The rest of the team should continue the process, one at a time. (Because this is a running game, make sure that the game area is clear of any protruding or sharp objects.)

Here are some instruction ideas to get you started:
• Draw a heart on someone's palm with red washable marker. Inside the heart, write "Jesus loves you."
• Tie a red bow in someone's hair to remind them of God's love.
• Pick out a Bible verse about love and read it to the rest of the team. Some verses to use could include: Matthew 19:19, Mark 12:30, Luke 6:27, and 1 Corinthians 13:13.
• Find out what every team member's middle name is and write them on a large piece of paper.
• Chew a piece of bubble gum, blow a bubble, and when it pops, shout "Jesus is alive!"
• Blow up a balloon and write on it, "Bursting with the good news that God's family is the best!" Then pop it.
• Cut out and draw a red heart with a cross on it for each member of your team. Distribute them.

Adjustment for Younger Ages

Make sure your instructions are things that can be done by kindergarten children such as: give someone a hug, put a sticker on someone's hand, tell someone with black hair a way that you can show love, and so on.

SINGING

Singing is a fun way to praise God. Make use of the songs included in this book, beginning on page 119. The songs in this book are also found on the *Bible Memory Toolbox* sing-along cassette tape. Be sure to learn the song "You Are a Chosen People," based on this week's Bible Blueprint Memory Verse. And remember to include some active songs to give kids an opportunity to move around.

CRITTER COUNTY STORY

The Tails of Two Cities

You probably all know by now that Critter County is a great place to live. But what you don't know is that there is one part of Critter County that is not so great. It's called Mole Alley. Why, the young critters are taught at a very early age not to even go near Mole Alley because it is such a dangerous place to be.

Back a generation or so ago, Critter County was safe and pleasant for all. The birds could actually nap on the back of the cats, and when kids went fishing, they would throw bread into the pond for the fish to eat. But then came a group of moles, four to be exact, from another county. And boy, were they hard to get along with. They often said mean things to the critters and sometimes stole from them. And they did not like the way the critters loved and took care of each other. This made the nice moles of Critter County sad. Eventually the four bad moles all moved to the same part of Critter County we now call Mole Alley.

Now Mole Alley has dozens of moles living there. And while not all the moles in Critter County are mean moles, the ones in the Mole Alley Club are. All the moles who belong to the club have the same hair cut and the same mark on their tails. It's a sad club because all they think about is themselves and how to get what they want. They like to scurry underground hiding food and pieces of jewelry they have stolen. If a small mouse gets too close to their territory, one of the teenage moles will go and nip at the legs of the poor little mouse until it runs away.

But in another part of Critter County, there's another club. This one meets at the Critter County Church. It's happy there. Very, very happy.

Every Monday morning, the club gets together to plan their week. Last Monday they decided to make a pot of lion chow for Liona Lou because she was sick in bed with the flu. While some of the women made the chow, Lester and Sydney changed the oil in Grandmother Mouse's car. Meanwhile, Lunchbox the lion cub, Beautiful the bunny, and Rascal the raccoon had a massive water balloon toss in the playground behind the church.

The two clubs never really had much contact . . . until last Friday night. You see, the Mole Alley Club decided to come and spy on the critters at the church club. They also had brought along some mean tricks to play on the critters. What they saw when they peeked through the windows was singing and laughter. At first, the moles made fun of the critters. But the more they watched, the more they wished that they could be happy like that, too.

You see, there wasn't much laughter in the Mole Alley Club unless someone was being made fun of. And there was very little happiness. Instead, the moles of Mole Alley were often fearful and angry. After watching the church club for quite some time, the leader mole told the other moles all to go home. There wouldn't be any tricks that night. But Sydney spotted three of the moles as they turned to leave, and he knew just what they had been up to. So he called everyone in his club together.

"I know many of you could be upset when I tell you that the Mole Alley moles have been spying on us. But we need to ask ourselves, 'What would Jesus do?'" And with that, Lunchbox held up his paw.

"I know Jesus would love them. So what can we do to be kind to them?" he asked.

"Well, Lunchbox," answered Sydney, "I think you have asked the right question. Does anyone have an idea?"

Liona Lou answered, "We could make them a big batch of mole rolls for breakfast."

"Great idea," answered Sydney. So they made a large basket of mole rolls and donut mole holes and the men delivered them to the door of the Mole Alley Clubhouse the very next morning. The note on top of the basket said, "Dear Moles. We hope you enjoyed seeing our club meeting. We have a wonderful time together because we try to help and love each other. We would like to invite you to come sometime. Here is a little gift from us to say, 'We care about you.' Sincerely, The Critter County Club."

Guess what happened? The Mole Alley Club moles loved the mole rolls and donut mole holes so much, and they were so moved by the kindness of the Critter County Club, that for two whole hours they sat around and tried to figure out who THEY could help. So if you ever see a mole hole in your yard, he may be coming to bring you a little gift from the Mole Alley Club.

Life Application Page

For Small Group Leaders

▶ **WEEK EIGHT** ◀

ON-THE-JOB TRAINING TOPIC:
Celebrate the best club ever

ACTION STEP:
Give thanks that Jesus is alive

BIBLE STORY:
Acts 9:1–19

MEMORY VERSE:
1 Peter 2:9 (NIV)

THINGS YOU'LL NEED:
- Copy of "Tips for Small Group Leaders" on pages 23–24
- Action Step / Training Topic poster
- Children's Journal
- Church Cutouts
- Adventure Prayer poster
- Children's Activity Book
- Pencils and paper

IN ADVANCE:
Make a tool-shaped poster of the Adventure Prayer on page 24. Also make tool-shaped posters of the Action Step and On-the-Job Training Topic, as well as church cutouts for kids to use as autograph sheets.

KID TALK

Show this week's Action Step and Training Topic. Invite the children to write a note or draw a picture for the pastor to thank him or her for helping to make the church a great place to be. Ask questions such as these to help children think about what they have learned in this Adventure.

- **How can we give thanks that Jesus is alive?**
- **What did we learn about helping others?**
- **Why is it important to meet with God in prayer and praise even in the hard times?**
- **What are some garbage thoughts and actions that we need to constantly clean out of our lives?**
- **What are some things our church (or church club) could do to encourage people in the neighborhood to visit church?**
- **What are some good things you could tell others about our church?**
- **What did you learn about becoming a good listener?**
- **What are some ways we can make the church or our church club a place where everyone can feel welcomed and loved?** (By using our tools or God-given talents well and encouraging others to use theirs; caring for and helping others; inviting new people to our church or church club; acting in a kind, caring, and respectful way; and so on.)

As a closing activity, provide each child with a cutout of a church and a pencil. (Older children may enjoy cutting out their own church if you have time.) Children could decorate their churches and then pass them on to other members of the group to sign and share a friendship comment. This is a nice reminder of your small group experience. (Younger children can sign their names and draw a picture.)

117

PRAYER TALK

Let's finish today by celebrating the best club ever. Let's close our Adventure Prayer today by thanking God for something that we enjoyed and/or learned during this Adventure.

Using your Adventure Prayer poster, read it with your group. Ask group members if they have any special prayer concerns or requests, and be sure to include them, also.

Small Group Tip

As your 50-Day Adventure draws to a close, help young people to also view today as a new start or a fresh beginning. They have journeyed a long way in building a church where everyone can feel welcomed and loved! Remind children that they have taken steps to strengthen their relationships with God along the way. Because of that they may be ready to do bigger and better things in God's name. Help children to remember that the process is ongoing and that we need to work on our Action Steps every day of our life!

We Ought to Love One Another

Theme 1—Based on 1 John 4:11 (NIV)

C. Wyrtzen

Dear friends, since God has loved — us, we ought to love one an—oth — er; Dear—

friends, since God has loved — us, — we ought to love one an — oth — er, —

First John, chap - ter four: e - le — ven - brings a message from the heart of hea — ven.

— Dear — friends, since God has—loved — us, — we ought to love one an—oth

— er. —

FINE

I Will Praise You, O Lord

Theme 2—Based on Psalm 9:1 (NIV)

C. Wyrtzen

I will praise you, I will praise you, O — Lord, O — Lord,

With all my heart, with all my heart; I will tell of your won — ders;

I will praise the Lord.

FINE

God Accepts Anyone

Theme 3—Based on Acts 10:35 (ICB)

C. Wyrtzen

God ac — cepts any — one who wor — ships him — and does what is right, — Acts ten: thir - ty five. — God ac — cepts any — one who wor - ships him. — It is not im - por -tant where a per - son comes from!

Use It!

Theme 4—Based on 1 Peter 4:10a

C. Wyrtzen

Use it, use it, use the gift — you have — re — ceived; yes, use it, use it, use it, for the — Lord. Serve one an - oth — er; What is that in your hand? — Sis- ters and bro — thers, — hear the — com — mand.

Be a Worker

Theme 5—Based on 2 Timothy 2:15b (ICB)

C. Wyrtzen

Be a wor - ker who is not ashamed —— of his work, of his work;

Be a wor - ker who is not ashamed —— of his work, of his work;

What is the work—? Read-ing God's Word. What is the work—? Un - der - stand - ing God's Word.

What is the work—? Do - ing God's Word, This is the work—. Yea!

Take Care of Their Needs

Theme 6—Based on Isaiah 58:10a (ICB)

C. Wyrtzen

For those who are hun —— gry,—— take care of their needs;—— For

those who are trou —— bled, —— take care —— of their needs. ——

Show the love —— of Je —— sus, —— give his heart a - way. ——

Hug the world a - round you;—— Take care of them in Je - sus' name. ——

It Is Good to Praise the Lord

Theme 7—Based on Psalm 92:1 (ICB)

C. Wyrtzen

You Are a Chosen People

Theme 8—Based on 1 Peter 2:9 (NIV)

C. Wyrtzen

Evaluation of the Grades 1–6 Curriculum for:
G. H. Construction Crew Children's Journal and
Critter County Clubhouse Children's Activity Book

Your feedback is important to us. Please take a few minutes to fill out this evaluation and send it to The Chapel Ministries at the address on the next page. We would appreciate your being as specific as possible. It might be a good idea to talk with the other adult leaders, with the children who participated, and with parents.

1. Which aspects of this curriculum did you find most helpful? What worked best with your children? Explain.

2. What did your adult leaders think about the various parts of the curriculum? How did the meeting plans work for them? Be specific.

3. How did the children respond to the program? What did they learn?

4. What suggestions do you have for improving this curriculum model for future 50-Day Adventures?

5. Was the *Bible Memory Toolbox* sing-along cassette tape helpful? If so, how?

6. Additional comments (use a separate sheet if necessary):

Name _____

Phone (_____) _____

Address _____

City _____

State/Prov_____ Zip/Code _____

Church Name and City _____

Please mail this evaluation to:
Editorial Department
The Chapel Ministries
Box 30, Wheaton, IL 60189

Cut on solid lines. **Fold** on dotted lines.

Cut ➝

Fold ➝

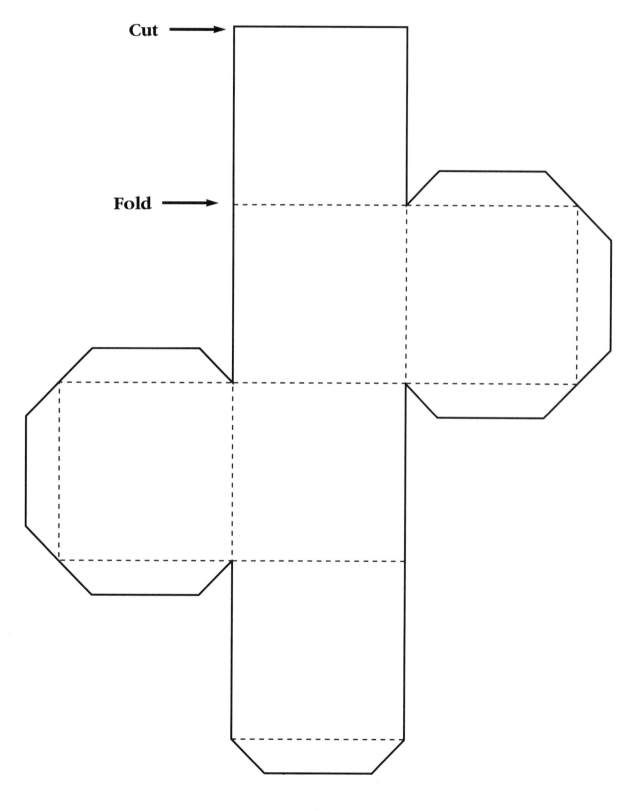

Sample Project and Activity Permission Slip

Customize this form to fit your situation.

Dear Parent,

For eight weeks beginning on *[date]*, your child will be participating in an exciting 50-Day Spiritual Adventure at Sunday school *[or children's church, church club, etc.]*. This program will include Bible-time projects along with creative Bible story presentations and life application groups *[and games]*.

Your child will have the chance to choose from a variety of Bible-time projects. Some of them involve sewing, carpentry, using hammers and nails, baking, dyeing cloth (using boiling water), and using sharp scissors. *[Customize this list to fit the projects you've chosen.]* Supervision will be provided at all times by adults or older teens.

[Some of the supervised games involve running and throwing activities.]

Please sign this permission slip and return it to *[name]* by *[date]*. If there are activities you would prefer your child did not participate in, please note them below.

Name of child ____

Please excuse from the following activities ______________________

____

Name of child ____

Please excuse from the following activities ______________________

____

Name of child ____

Please excuse from the following activities ______________________

____

Parent's signature ____

Date ____

Item	Title	Price Each	Qty	Discount Price**	Total
	G. H. Construction Crew				
2730	*G. H. Construction Crew* Children's Journal (3–6)	$6.00	____	_____	_____
2740	*Critter County® Clubhouse* Activity Book (K–2)	$6.00	____	_____	_____
450X	*Critter County Clubhouse* Children's Scripture Memory Tape	$6.00	____	_____	_____
450Z	*Bible Memory Toolbox* Curriculum Sing-along Tape	$6.00	____	_____	_____
	Other Adventures				
3610	*Adventure Gear for God's Kids* Grades 1–6 Leader's Guide & Sing-along Tape	$30.00	____		_____
2630	*Adventure Gear for God's Kids* Children's Journal (3–6)	$6.00	____	_____	_____
2640	*Pack Up My Backpack* Activity Book (K–2)	$6.00	____	_____	_____
450S	*Pack Up My Backpack* Children's Scripture Memory Tape	$6.00	____	_____	_____
3506	*Facing the Fearigators* Children's Church Leader's Guide & Sing-along Tape	$20.00	____		_____
2540	*Facing the Fearigators* Activity Book (K–2)	$6.00	____	_____	_____

Subtotal _____

Add 10% for UPS shipping/handling ($4.00 minimum) _____

Canadian or Illinois residents add 7% GST/sales tax _____

Total (subtotal + shipping + tax) _____

Here's my donation to help support the work of The Chapel Ministries _____

Total Amount Enclosed _____

Ship my order to:

Name _____

Church Name_____

Street Address*_____City _____

State/Prov_____ Zip/Code _____Phone (____)_____

*Note: UPS will not deliver to a PO box.

Mail this order form with your check made payable to:
The Chapel Ministries, Box 30, Wheaton, IL 60189-0030
In Canada: Box 2000, Waterdown, ON L0R 2H0

For Discover, VISA, or MasterCard orders call 1-800-224-2735 (U.S.) or 1-800-461-4114 (Canada).

**Quantity Discounts: You may combine the first three items on this order form to determine your quantity discount price (*G. H. Construction, Clubhouse* Activity Book, and *Clubhouse* Scripture Memory Tape). 10–99: $4.95/ 100–299: $4.75 / 300+: $4.50. The same quantity discounts may be applied to the journals, activity books, and children's Scripture memory tapes for other Adventures.

CLG497